Companion to

Glitterati

Portraits & Jewelry from Colonial Latin America at the Denver Art Museum

Donna Pierce & Julie Wilson Frick

Contents

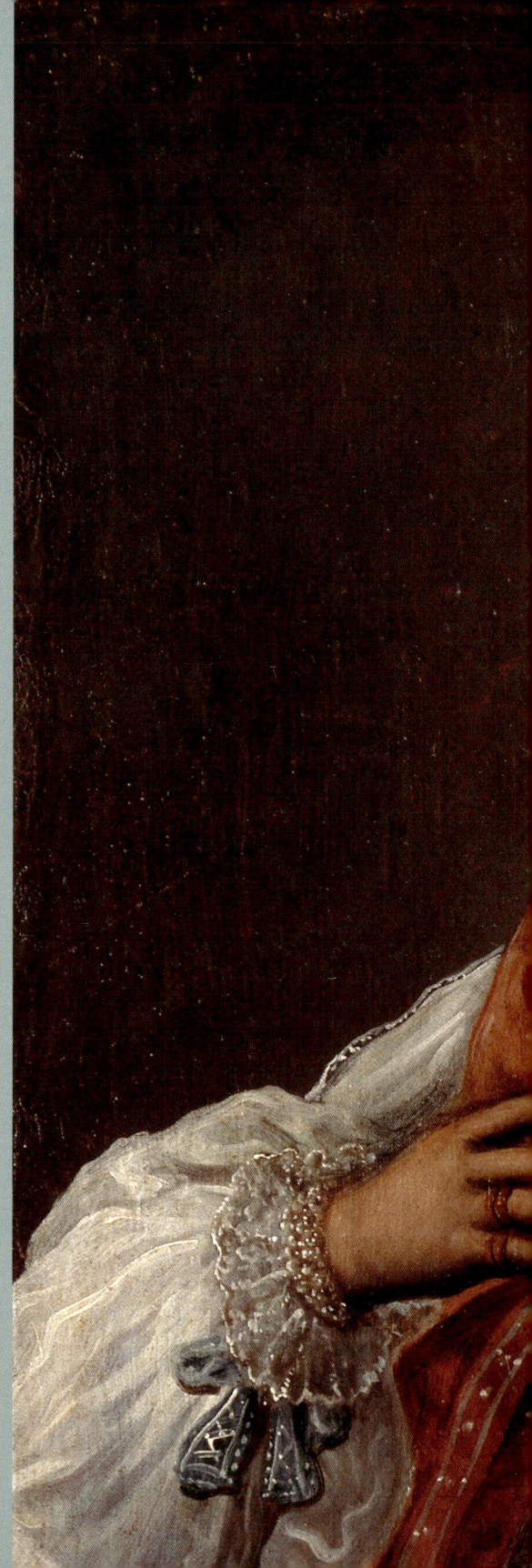

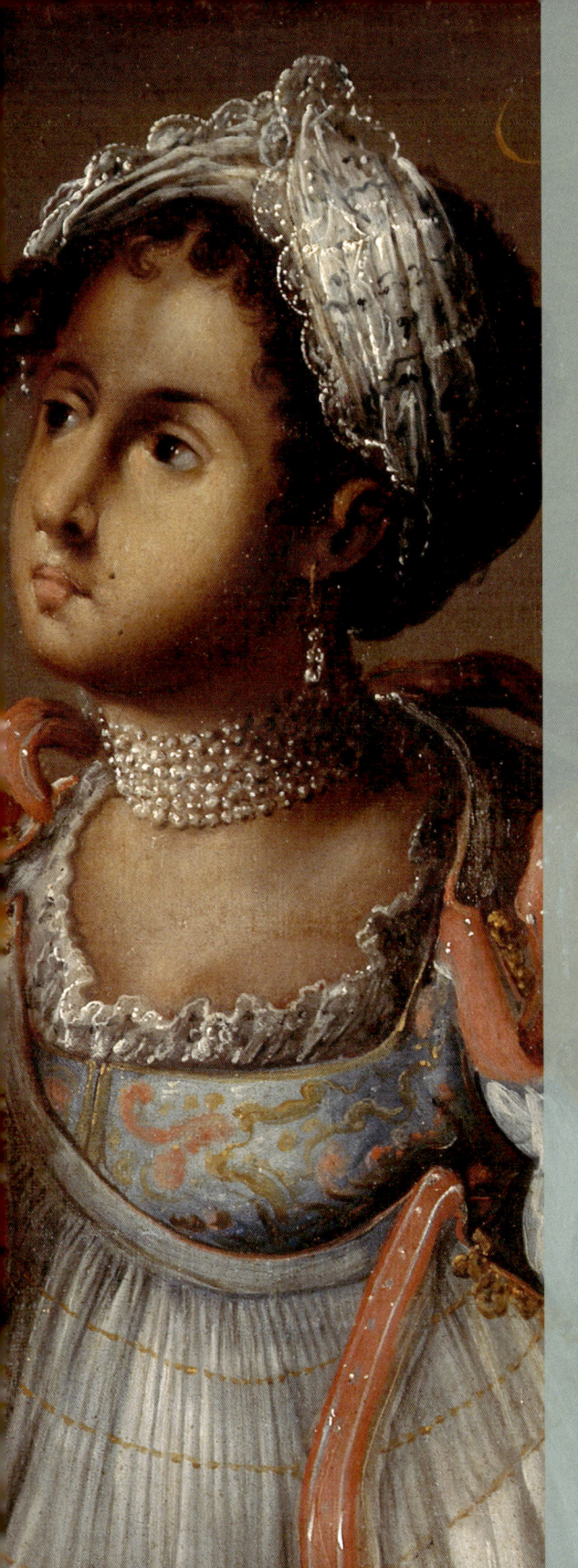

Dedicated with
affection and
gratitude to
Jan Mayer
and to the
memory of
Frederick Mayer
for their vision,
passion, and
generosity

Foreword

The Spanish Colonial collection at the Denver Art Museum is the most comprehensive of its kind in the United States and one of the best in the world. Not only does it contain outstanding examples of painting, sculpture, furniture, and decorative arts from all over Latin America during the time of the Spanish colonies (1521–1850), it also includes spectacular examples of lacquerware, personal effects, silver and gold work, jewelry, and portraiture.

The museum's Spanish Colonial collection began with Anne Evans's 1936 gift of a group of santos from the U.S. Southwest, but it was not until 1968 that the New World Department was established, bringing pre-Columbian and Spanish Colonial objects from Latin America together. Immediately the New World Department began receiving the Frank Barrows Freyer Memorial Collection of colonial art from Peru and Bolivia, assembled by María Engracia Freyer during the 1920s. The spectacular 1990 gift of the Stapleton Foundation's extensive collection of colonial art from Ecuador, Colombia, and Venezuela, a donation made possible by the Renchard family of Washington, D.C., greatly expanded the Spanish Colonial collection.

Since the early 1980s the department has flourished through the interest and support of longtime museum trustee Frederick Mayer and his wife, Jan. With their financial support, the New World collections were reorganized and reinstalled in the Jan and Frederick Mayer Galleries of Pre-Columbian and Spanish Colonial Art in 1993. Later their enlightened endowment gift underwrote the department's two curatorial positions and administrative costs. They also founded the Frederick and Jan Mayer Center for Pre-Columbian and Spanish Colonial Art at the Denver Art Museum, dedicated to increasing awareness and promoting scholarship by sponsoring academic activities including annual symposia, fellowships, study trips, research projects, conservation, and publications.

Over the years the Mayers built their own collections of pre-Columbian and Spanish Colonial art intended to benefit the New World Department. After the untimely death of Frederick in 2007, Jan Mayer began gifting their outstanding Spanish Colonial art collection to the museum. In celebration of the final stages of that series of gifts, we are pleased to dedicate this exhibition and publication, *Glitterati: Portraits and Jewelry from Colonial Latin America*, to her. She is our jewel.

Christoph Heinrich
Frederick and Jan Mayer Director
Denver Art Museum

Acknowledgments

Many people work behind the scenes to mount an exhibition and produce a publication. We would like to acknowledge the hands-on staff of the museum's Conservation Department for their expertise in preparing the works for exhibition, in particular Gina Laurin, Pam Skiles, and Courtney Murray, as well as Steve Osborne and Nick Donaldson for making the inconspicuous mounts that show off the jewels to perfection. The Collections staff worked behind the scenes to make the objects accessible during the exhibition preparation process. Kara Kudzma headed up exhibition planning and installation with aplomb and calm, while the installation crew, including John Lupe, Kevin Hester, Ethan Tuers, Jeff Keene, David Griesheimer, and Laura Bennison, handled the installation with their usual good humor and outstanding professionalism. Heather Nielsen and her team from the Department of Learning and Engagement provided the content for the in-gallery iPads installed by Cordelia Taylor. Special thanks go to Laura Caruso, director of publications, for her editorial magic, and to Amy Schell for designing the elegant labels.

We gratefully acknowledge the contributions and encouragement of New World staff Anne Tennant, research associate; Jana Gottshalk, former curatorial assistant; Jesse Laird Ortega, curatorial assistant; Sabena Kull, research intern; and Margaret Young-Sánchez, Frederick and Jan Mayer Curator of Pre-Columbian Art. Museum photographers Jeff Wells and Christina Jackson executed the photography seen in these pages. Digital mapmaker Fabrice Weexsteen offered technical and scholarly knowledge in the creation of the maps. Thanks are due to the staff of O'Neil Printing for production of this volume and to the University of Oklahoma Press for distribution. For many years of research collaboration, we thank our colleagues Michael Brown and Ann Daley.

We are indebted to Frederick and Jan Mayer for their support of the New World Department through their generous endowment, program funding, founding of the Mayer Center for Pre-Columbian and Spanish Colonial Art, donations to the permanent collection, and years of genuine friendship.

Donna Pierce
Frederick and Jan Mayer Curator of Spanish Colonial Art /
Head of the New World Department

Julie Wilson Frick
Mayer Center Program Coordinator / Junior Scholar
New World Department

Spanish Colonial Portraits and Jewelry at the Denver Art Museum

Donna Pierce and Julie Wilson Frick

During many years of working with the Spanish Colonial collection at the Denver Art Museum, we had looked with envy at the numerous and beautiful pieces of gold jewelry from South America in the Stapleton Collection. We were well aware that the Mayer Collection held the largest selection in the United States of exquisite nun's badges, small paintings on copper worn as jewelry by nuns in colonial Mexico. Most of these jewels had never been exhibited, and we wished for an opportunity to display them.

As the Denver Art Museum began planning for a major exhibition of Cartier jewelry for 2014, we decided to take advantage of the theme and re-investigate our own collection of Spanish Colonial jewelry as well as portraits showing sitters wearing such jewelry. Once we focused on the jewels in paintings, we were delighted to find more examples than we expected. Our research resulted in the exhibition *Glitterati: Portraits and Jewelry from Colonial Latin America*, which opened in the Spanish Colonial galleries December 6, 2014. This publication serves as a companion to the *Glitterati* exhibition and, in a broader sense, to the collection of Spanish Colonial jewelry and portraiture at the Denver Art Museum.

Two core art collections made this project possible.

The collection of the Stapleton Foundation of Latin American Colonial Art was gifted by the Renchard family of Washington, D.C., in 1990. The art was acquired by the intrepid Daniel C. Stapleton between 1895 and 1914 when he worked in Ecuador, Colombia, and Venezuela, overseeing plantations and emerald mines. En route he acquired objects of colonial art that he shipped to his fiancée in Nebraska. After the outbreak of World War I, he moved with his wife and daughter to Washington, D.C., where they lived with many of these objects in their home. Today, colonial art from this region is exceptionally rare outside of country of origin, and, thanks to the Renchard family, the Denver Art Museum has the best collection of its kind.

Glitterati was also made possible by the Frederick and Jan Mayer Collection of Spanish Colonial Art. The Mayers worked closely with New World curator Robert Stroessner from 1968 until his death in 1991 to build a collection of Mexican colonial art to complement the previously gifted Freyer Collection from Peru and Bolivia and the Stapleton Collection. When we came to the museum in the late 1990s, we began to work with the Mayers to identify holes in the overall collection and make targeted acquisitions to fill those, as well as to acquire secular material such as portraits, genre paintings, and decorative arts to balance the religious objects already in the collection. The Mayer/ Denver Art Museum collection now comprises the largest holdings of Mexican colonial art outside of Mexico. Many of those pieces, particularly portraits, are showcased in the *Glitterati* exhibition and in this volume.

Objects gifted by other donors round out the exhibition and publication, thanks to the generosity of María Engracia Freyer, Lorraine and Harley Higbie, Mr. and Mrs. James Jeter, Dr. Mary Lanius, Frances Lowe Scott, Dr. Belinda Straight, Robert Stroessner, Mrs. Leroy Schwartz, Marilynn and Carl Thoma, Jim and Marybeth Vogelzang, and Alianza de las Artes Americanas. David and Boo Butler kindly lent their lovely painting to the project.

These generous "glitterati" of the modern era have made it possible to showcase the exquisite pieces of jewelry worn centuries ago by the "glitterati" of colonial Latin America.

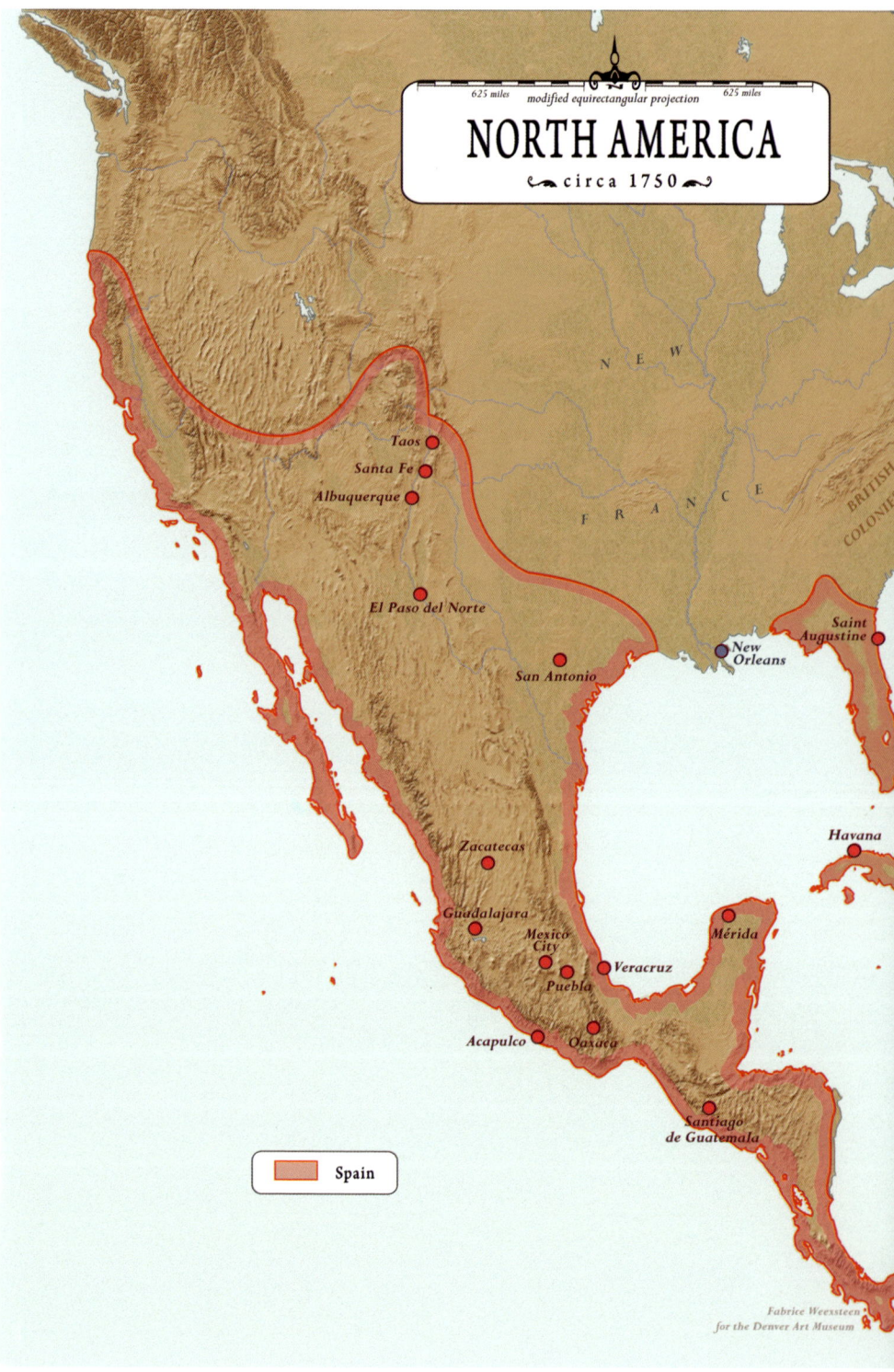

625 miles   modified equirectangular projection   625 miles

NORTH AMERICA

circa 1750

N E W

F R A N C E

BRITISH
COLONIES

Taos

Santa Fe

Albuquerque

El Paso del Norte

San Antonio

New
Orleans

Saint
Augustine

Zacatecas

Havana

Guadalajara

Mexico
City

Mérida

Veracruz

Puebla

Acapulco

Oaxaca

Santiago
de Guatemala

Spain

*Fabrice Weessteen
for the Denver Art Museum*

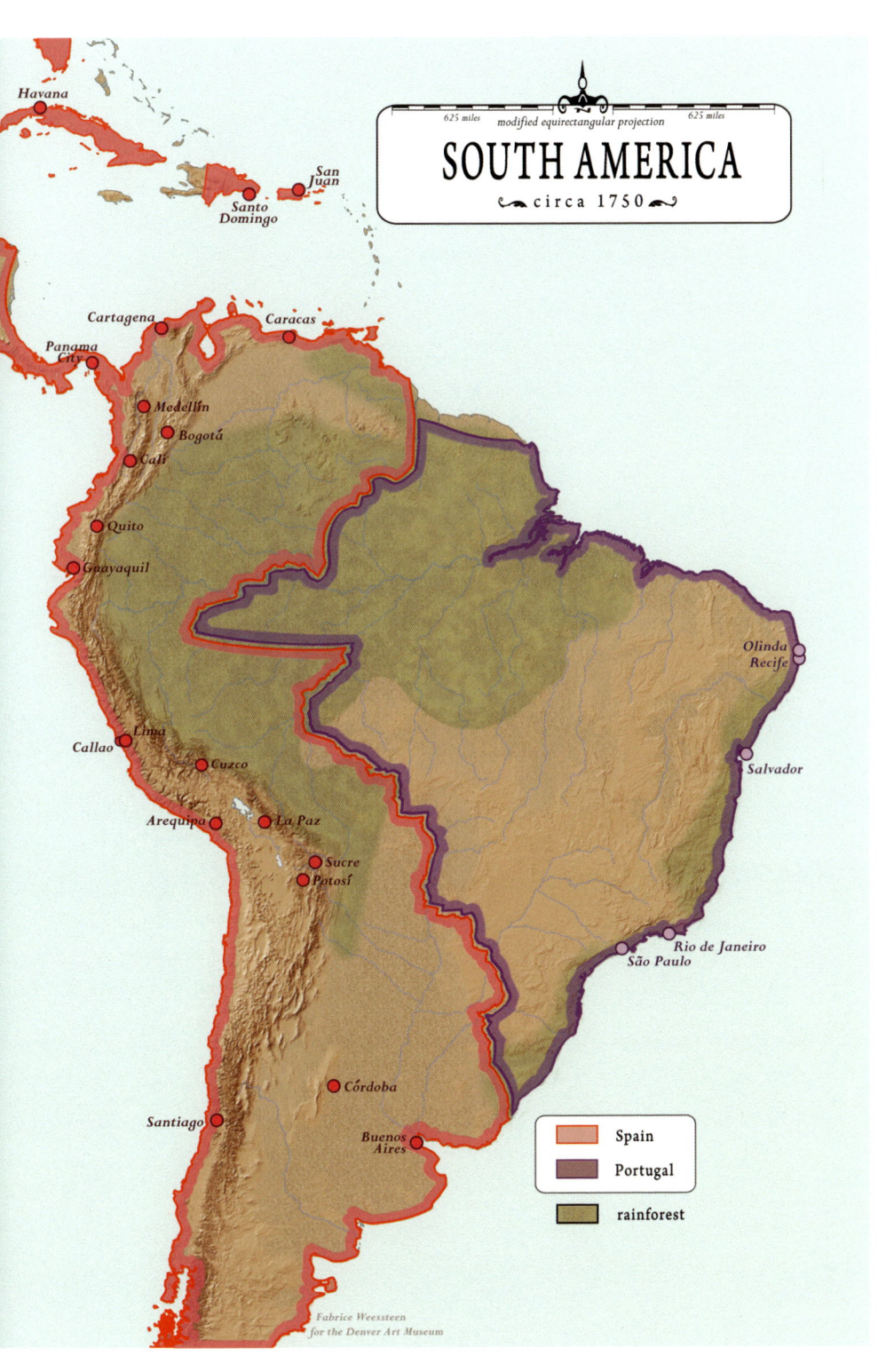

Havana

San Juan

Santo Domingo

Cartagena

Caracas

Panama City

Medellín

Bogotá

Cali

Quito

Guayaquil

Olinda
Recife

Callao

Lima

Cuzco

Salvador

Arequipa

La Paz

Sucre

Potosí

Rio de Janeiro

São Paulo

Córdoba

Santiago

Buenos Aires

A

625 miles   modified equirectangular projection   625 miles

SOUTH AMERICA

circa 1750

Spain

Portugal

rainforest

Fabrice Weexsteen
for the Denver Art Museum

Old World and New World Glitterati

Moctezuma has all things, whether on land or sea, modeled very realistically in either gold or silver and jewels or feathers with such perfection they seem almost real.

— Hernán Cortés, Spanish explorer of Mexico, 1520

Many residents of colonial Latin America (1521–1850) had the means to deck themselves out in fashionable clothing and glittering jewelry. They were, in a sense, the glitterati or celebrities of their day. Economic prosperity and plentiful raw materials such as metals and precious and semiprecious stones made such elegance possible.

When Spanish explorers arrived in the New World in the early 1500s they found abundant gold and silver. American Indians already had a long tradition of metalworking. Soon silversmiths from Spain immigrated to the Americas and introduced European styles that merged with native traditions to produce unique pieces.

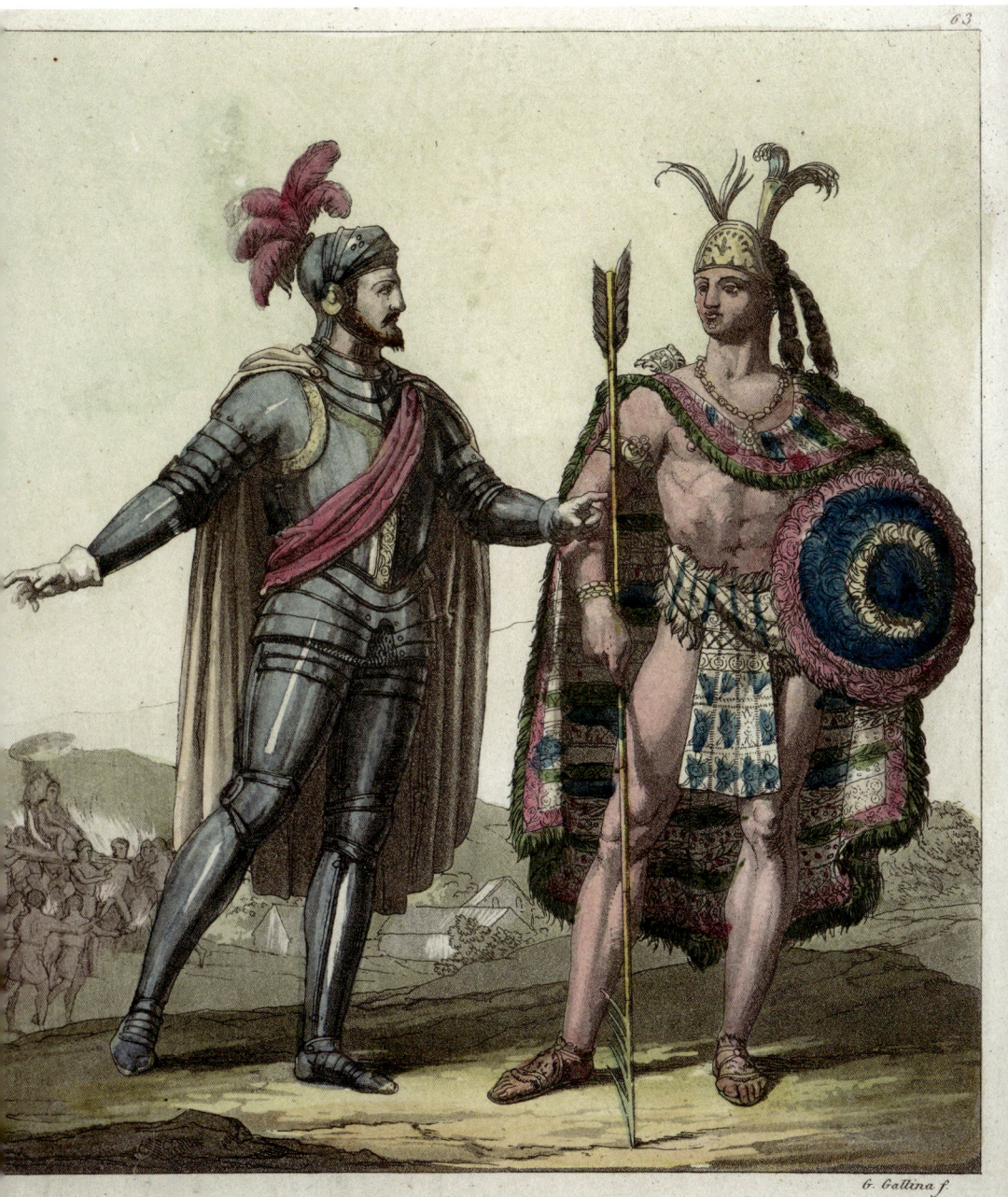

Gallo Gallina
(1796–1874)

Encounter of Hernán Cortés and Moctezuma

Milan (Italy), mid 1800s
Handcolored engraving on paper
6½ x 5½ in.
Gift of Frederick and Jan Mayer;
2000.353

Although this engraving dates from the nineteenth century, it is based on earlier images depicting both Hernán Cortés, conqueror of Mexico, and Moctezuma, the last emperor of the Aztecs. Here, as in the earlier images, Moctezuma is seen wearing an elaborate feather cape and loincloth and holding a feathered shield. Documents from the era describe him with golden sandals and arm bands, as seen here. He also wears a necklace of beads that appear to be coral and jade or turquoise. Both men wear headgear with plumes: Cortés wears a military helmet made of iron, whereas Moctezuma is crowned with a golden diadem that indicates his status as emperor.

Inca Rulers (set of sixteen)

Peru, late 1800s
Oil paint on canvas
25½ x 19½ in. (each)
Gift of Dr. Belinda Straight; 1977.45

This set of paintings shows the lineage of rulership in Peru, beginning with Manco Capac and his wife, Mama Occollo (opposite), the founders of the Inca royal dynasty, and ending with Atahuallpa, the last emperor of the Incas, and Francisco Pizarro (page 17), the Spanish conqueror who arrived in 1532.

The Inca kings wear royal headdresses (*llautu*) and tunics (*uncu*) covered with geometric patterns. Mama Occollo wears the traditional women's mantle (*lliclla*) held in place by a *ttipqui* pin (see pages 18–19) inserted diagonally in front.

During the Spanish Colonial period, families who could prove they were of noble blood, either Inca or Spanish, could be exempt from paying taxes and entitled to special privileges. As a result, Inca ruler paintings were proudly displayed in the homes of descendants of Inca nobility as a way of expressing indigenous identity and documenting lineage. This set of portraits was painted in the late 1800s, more than three hundred years after the arrival of Pizarro in Peru.

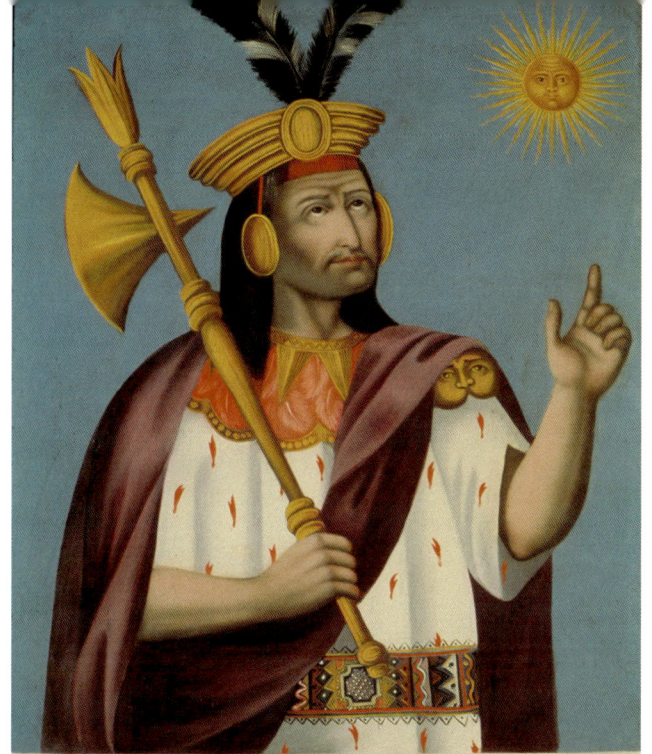

MANCCO CCAPAC, INCA 1.° D. PERU.

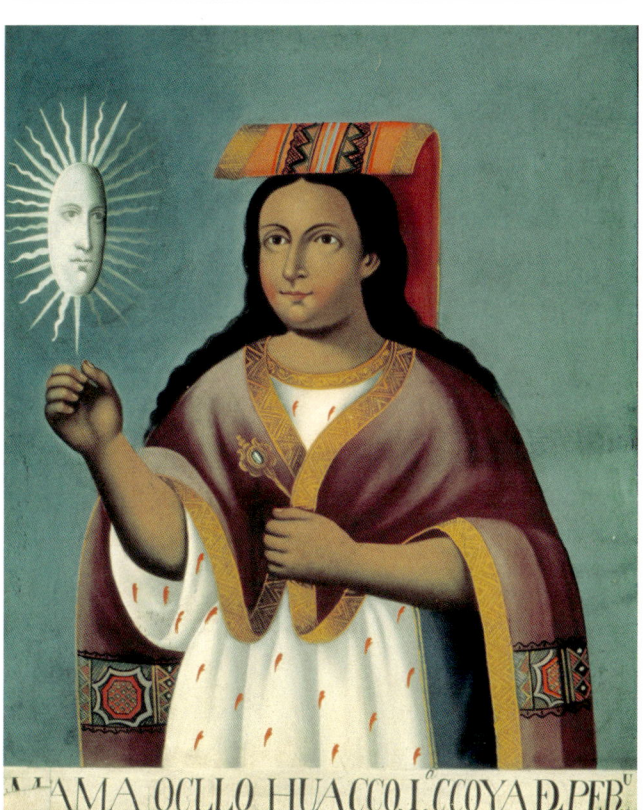

LLAMA OCLLO HUACCO, 1.° CCOYA D. PER.

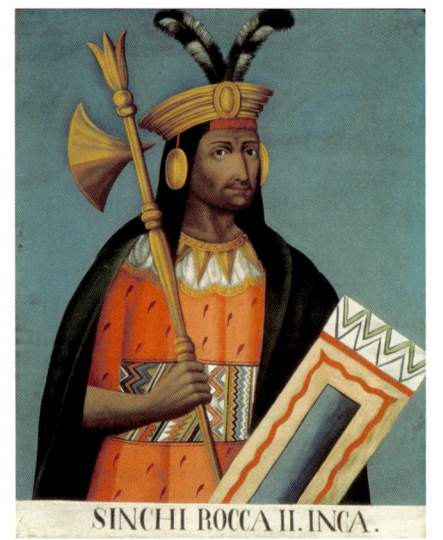

SINCHI ROCCA II. INCA.

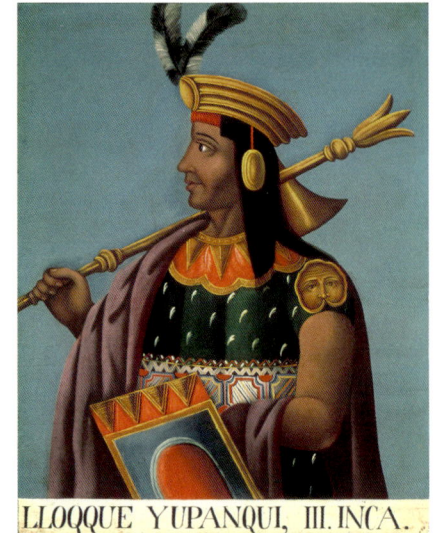

LLOQQUE YUPANQUI, III. INCA.

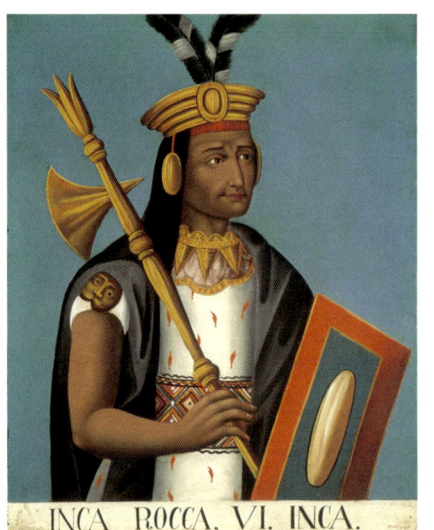

INCA ROCCA, VI. INCA.

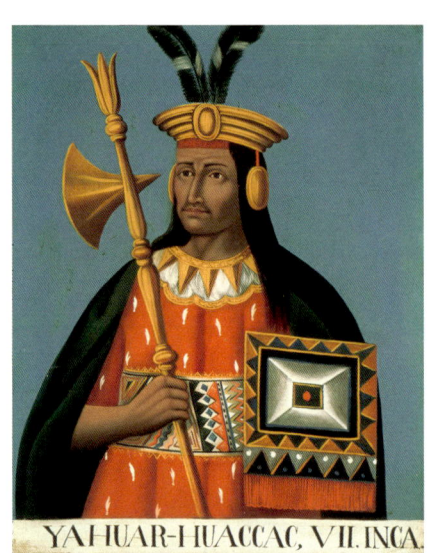

YAHUAR-HUACCAC, VII. INCA.

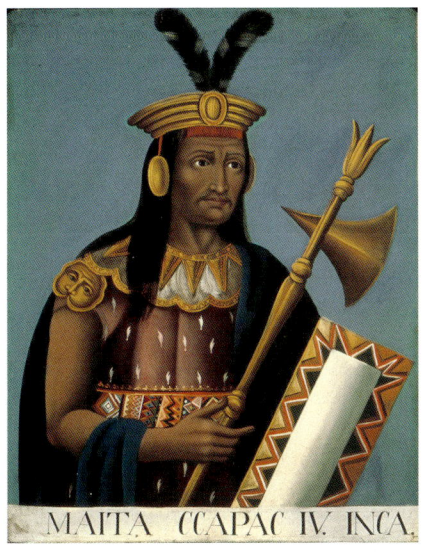

MAITA CCAPAC IV. INCA.

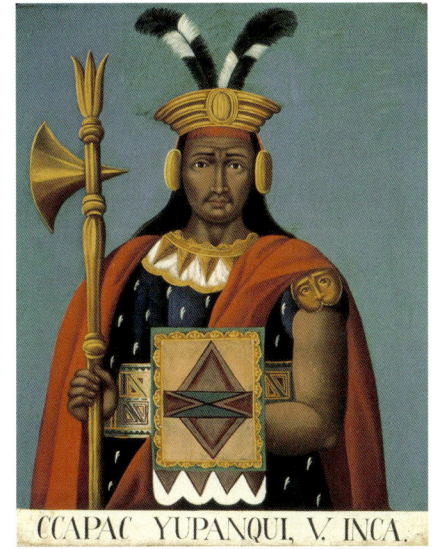

CCAPAC YUPANQUI, V. INCA.

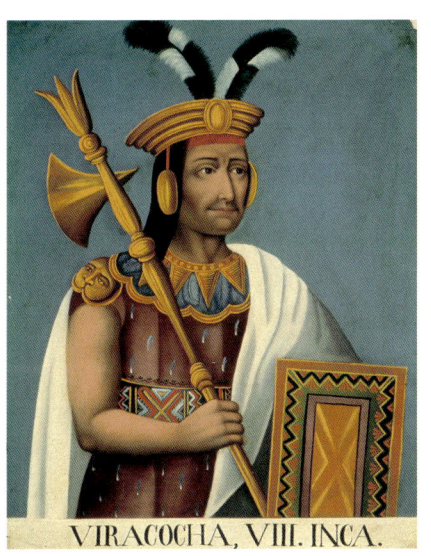

VIRACOCHA, VIII. INCA.

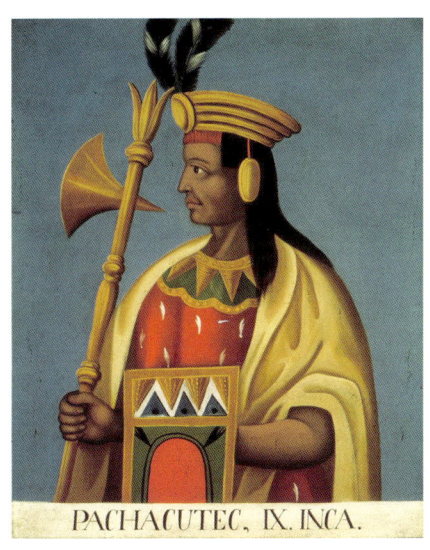

PACHACUTEC, IX. INCA.

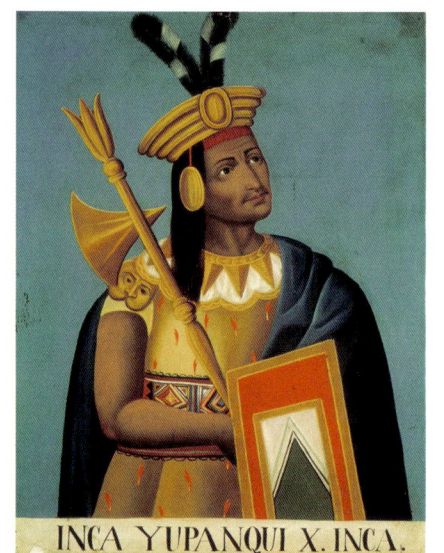

INCA YUPANQUI X. INCA.

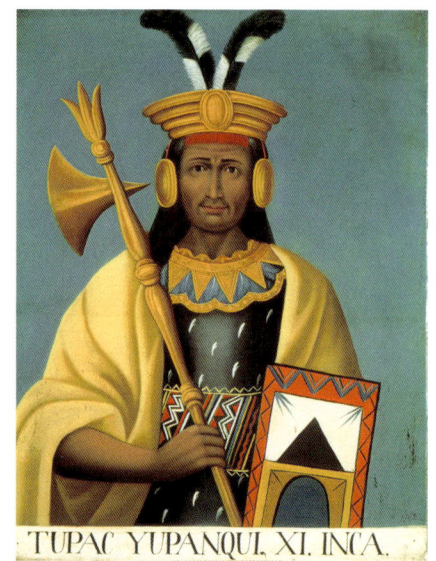

TUPAC YUPANQUI, XI. INCA.

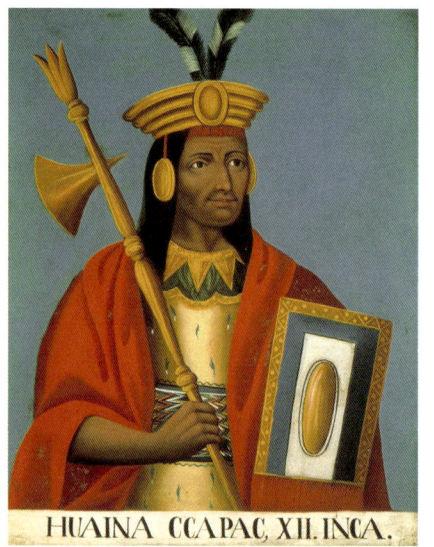

HUAINA CCAPAC, XII. INCA.

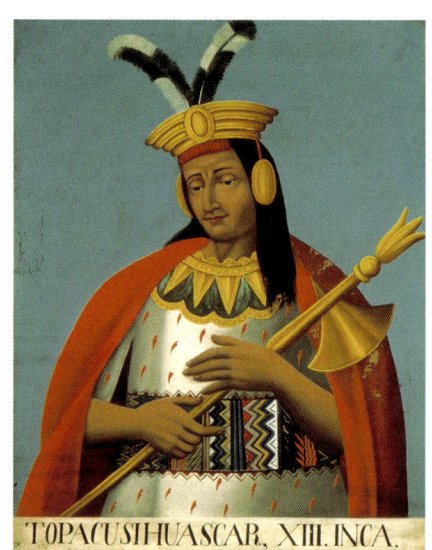

TOPACUSIHUASCAR, XIII. INCA.

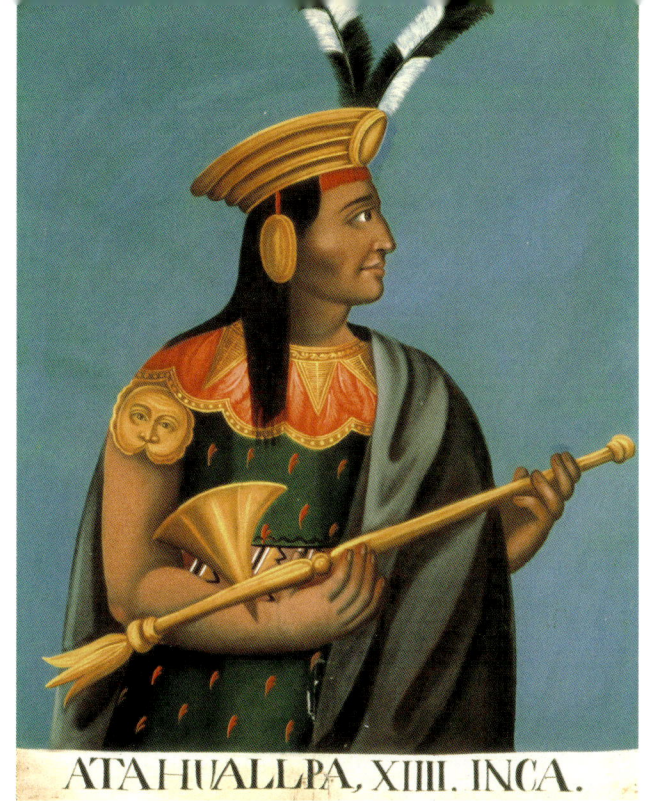

ATAHUALLPA, XIIII. INCA.

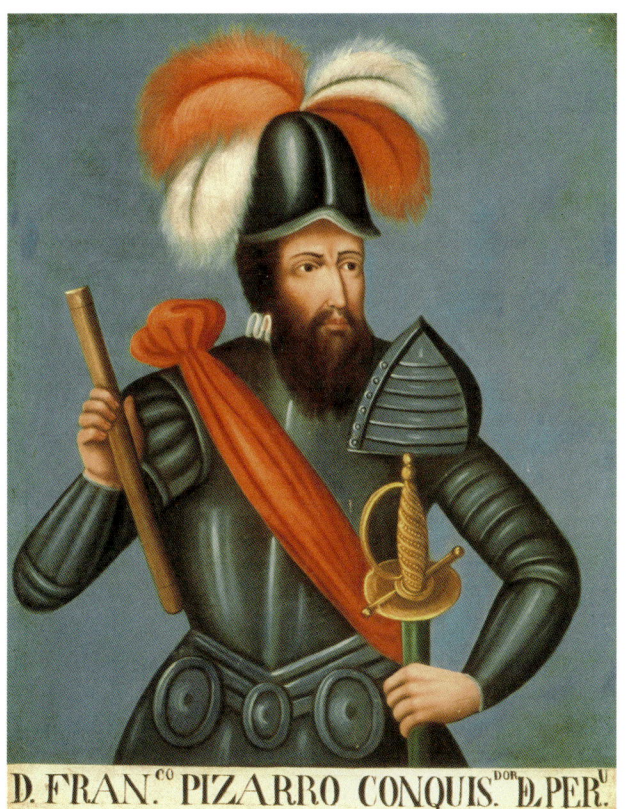

D. FRAN.^{co} PIZARRO CONQUIS.^{DOR} D. PER.^U

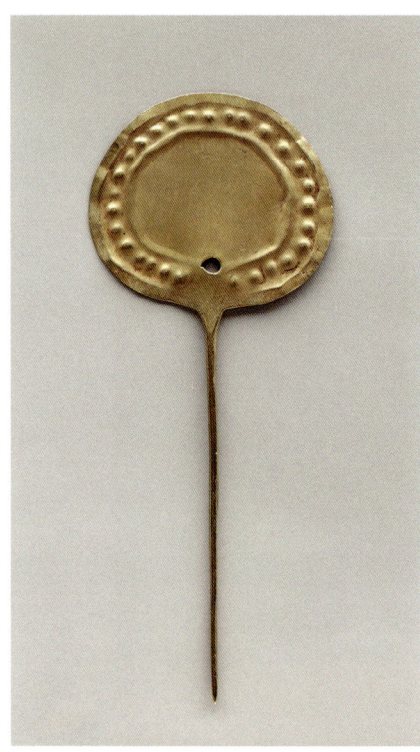

Tupu Pin (one of a pair)

Inca
Peru, Chile, or Bolivia, 1400–1500
Gold
5⅞ x 2¼ x 1/16 in.
Anonymous gift; 1995.318.1, .2

Tupus, metal stick pins with flat, round heads, were used throughout the Inca empire to fasten women's tubular dresses at the shoulders. These pins were worn one on each shoulder and positioned vertically, with the heads down.

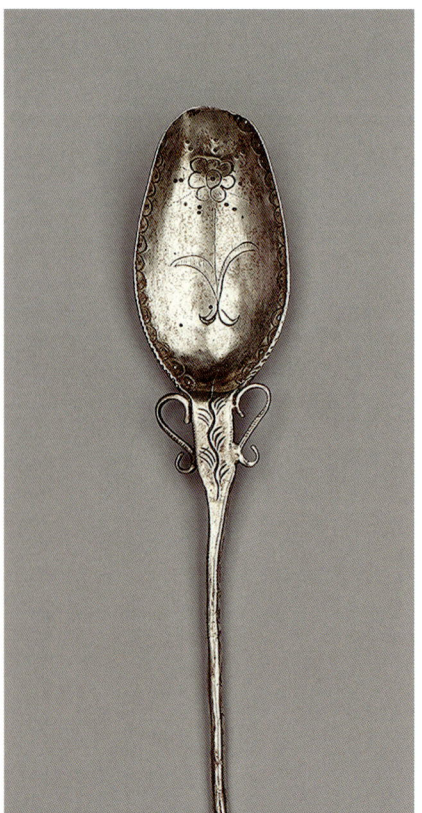

Ttipqui Pin

Colombia or Ecuador, 1700s
Silver
13¾ x 2⅛ x 1⅜ in.
Gift of the Stapleton Foundation of Latin American Colonial Art, made possible by the Renchard family; 1990.419

After European contact, many *tupu* and *ttipqui* pins were made out of silver spoons or incorporated spoon designs, as seen here. It is hard to tell them apart today, but *ttipquis* tend to have longer shafts than *tupus*. The two types of pins became more like each other during the colonial period when tubular dresses went out of fashion.

(right)

Ttipqui Pin

Peru, 1800s
Silver-plated copper
9½ in. long
Gift of Mrs. LeRoy Schwartz; 1954.156

Single *ttipqui* pins were inserted diagonally to fasten mantles or capes
at the neck. Sun and moon imagery,
which figures prominently in both
pre-Columbian and Christian art, is
often seen on pins made during the
colonial period.

(below)

Ttipqui Pin

Peru, 1800s
Silver
9 x 2¼ in.
Gift of Dr. Mary Lanius; 2008.844

This pin is incised with a double-
headed eagle, the symbol of the
Hapsburg kings, who ruled Spain in
the 1500s and 1600s.

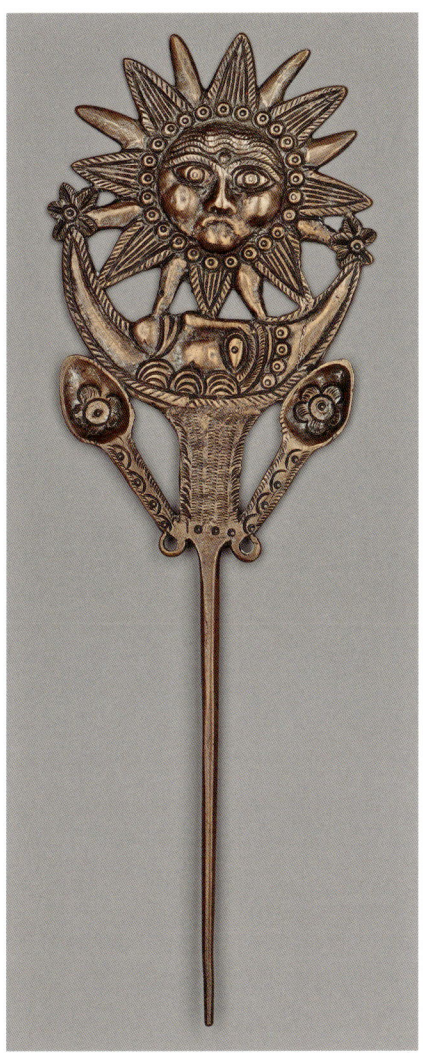

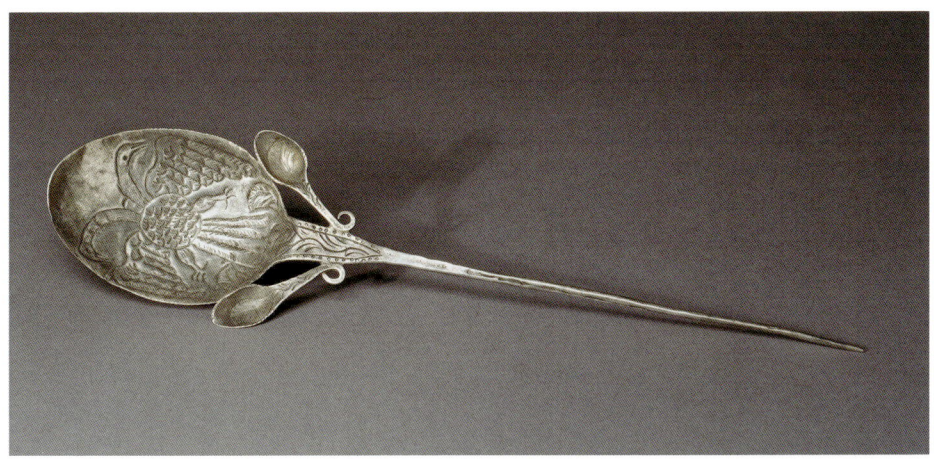

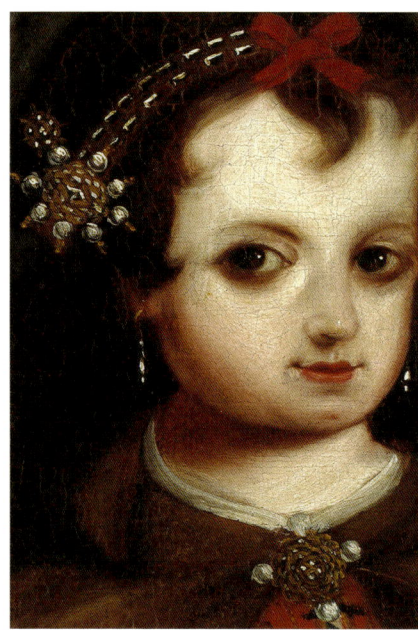

(opposite, and detail left)

Virgin Mary Spinning

Spain, about 1700
Oil paint on canvas
25 x 21 in.
Gift of Engracia Freyer Dougherty for
the Frank Barrows Freyer Collection;
1969.353

Images of the Virgin Mary as a child spinning yarn became popular in Spain and Peru in the 1600s. The Virgin's skirt, embroidered sleeves, and laced bodice are in the European style. Her cloak, held together by a circular jewel, recalls both Spanish capes and the Inca *lliclla* mantle fastened by a *ttipqui* pin, as seen in the previous pages.

During conservation treatment, a crochet needle was found between the canvas and the stretcher of the painting. It was likely placed there by a devoted former owner as an offering to the Virgin Mary.

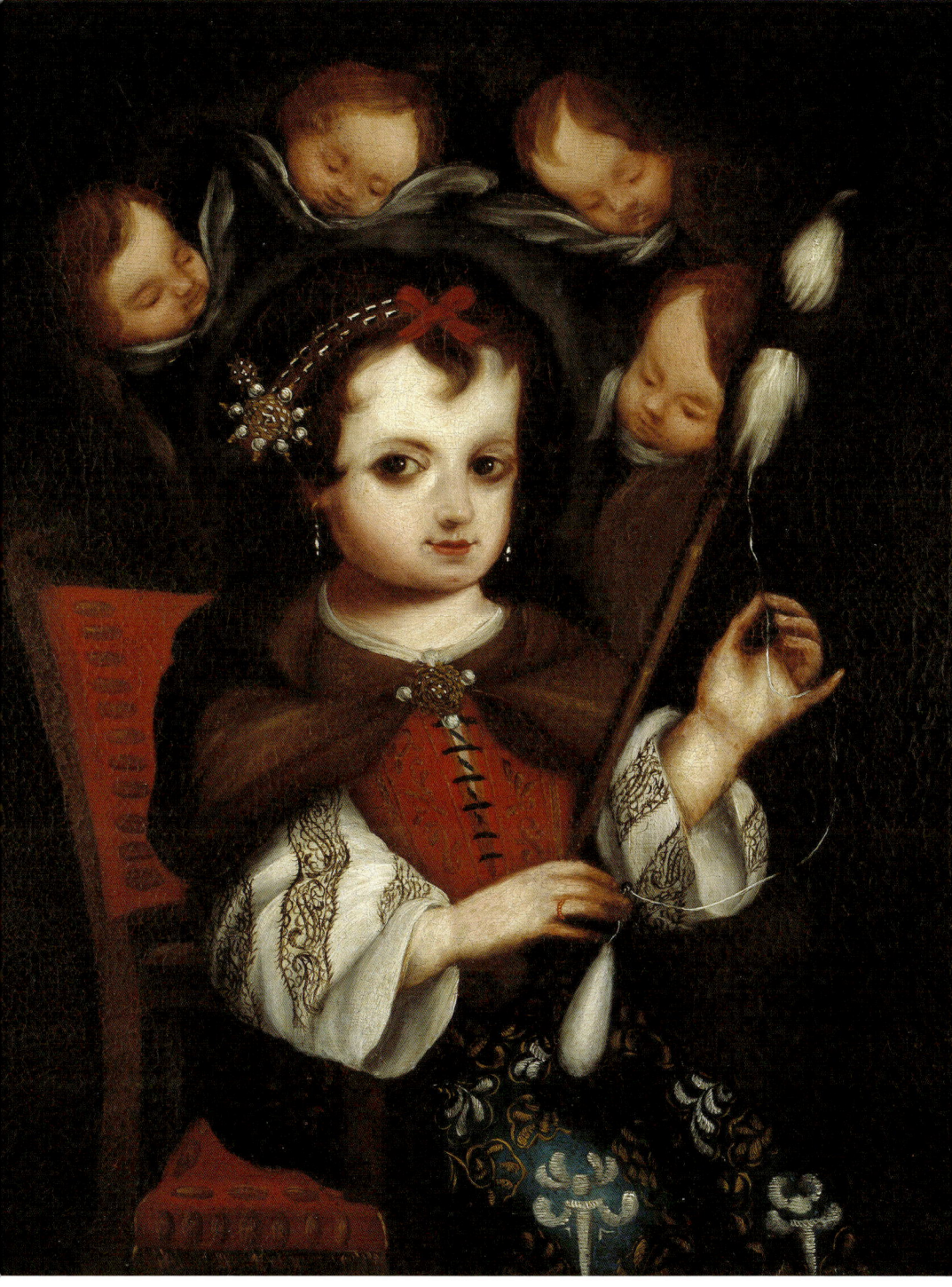

Abundance in the Americas

I have seen the objects brought from the new land: a sun of solid gold; also a moon of pure silver, and am amazed by the subtle inventiveness of the men of far off lands.

— Albrecht Dürer, German artist, speaking of Aztec art from Mexico, 1520

Prior to the arrival of Europeans, native peoples of Latin America mined jade, emeralds, and other gemstones, often fashioning them into beads. Around 1600, the Spanish began mining in Muzo, Colombia, extracting extremely high-quality emeralds that came to be coveted around the world.

Pearls and coral were so readily available in Mexico and South America that women of all classes wore multistrand pearl and coral bracelets, necklaces, and earrings. By the 1720s diamonds had been discovered in the Portuguese colony of Brazil, and diamond jewelry became popular throughout Europe and the New World.

Gemstones and ivory made their way to the New World from Asia on the Manila galleon trade ships, which sailed the Pacific from 1565 to 1815. Glass stones from Central Europe and fake stones made locally were also among the materials that jewelers had at hand.

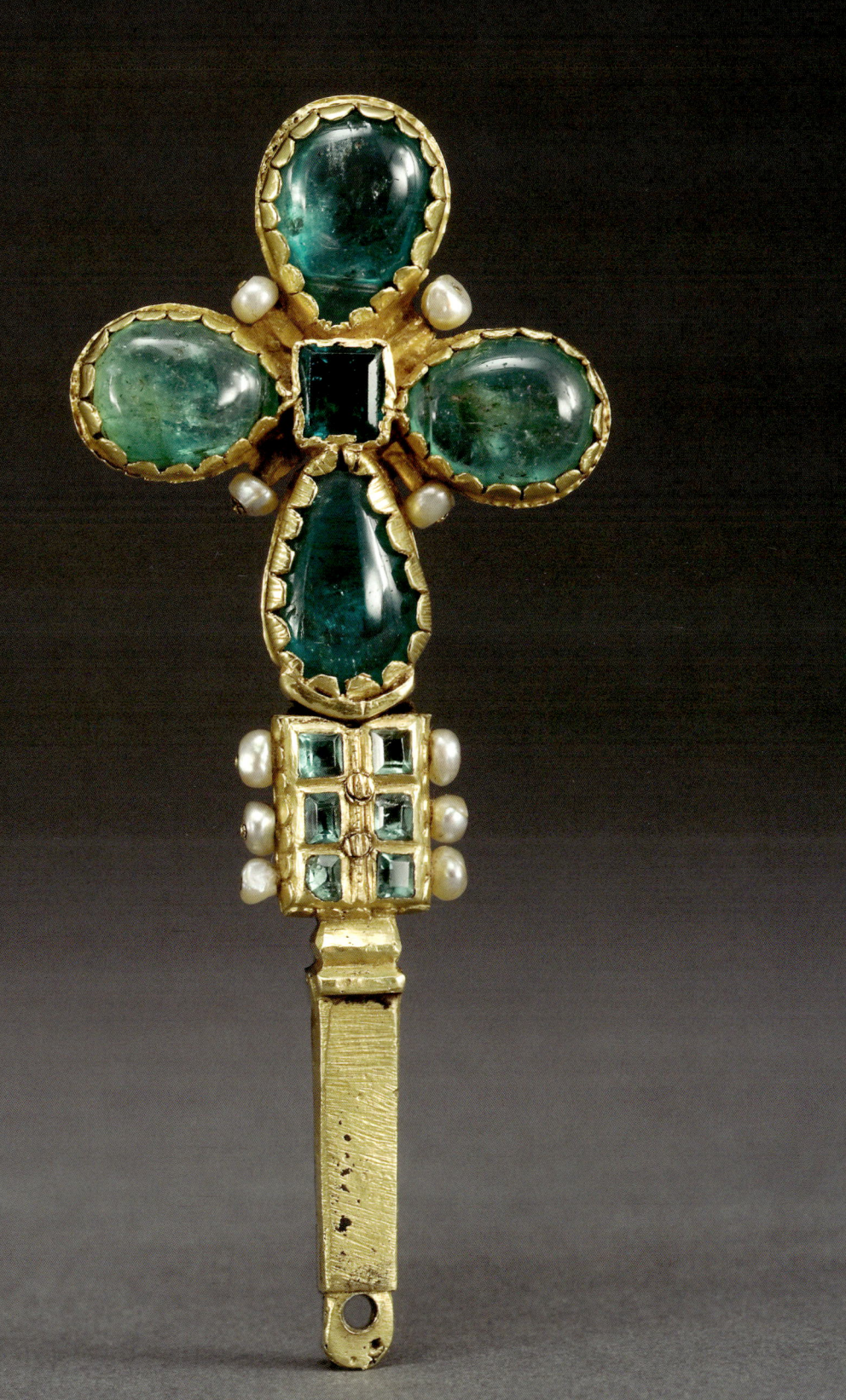

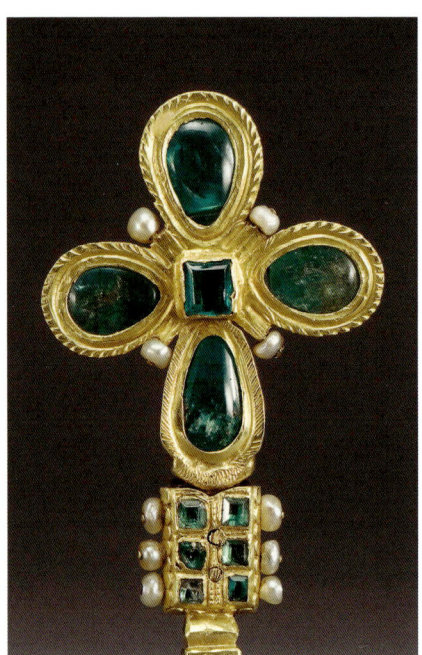

Cross Finial

Colombia, about 1600
Gold, emeralds, and pearls
4 x 1½ in.
Gift of the Stapleton Foundation of
Latin American Colonial Art, made pos-
sible by the Renchard family; 1990.526

This cross was likely made to sit
on top of a crown and is embellished with ten pearls, perhaps
from Venezuela, and seven faceted
emeralds of exceptional quality,
probably from the Muzo mines of
Colombia. Under magnification, the
four large oval emeralds show signs
of being carved originally with
stone tools, indicating they may
be pre-Columbian beads that were
refashioned during the colonial
period.

(left)

Cross Pendant

Colombia or Ecuador, 1800s
Gold
3 x 2¼ in.
Gift of the Stapleton Foundation of
Latin American Colonial Art, made pos-
sible by the Renchard family; 1990.624

Filigree, or metal lace, as it was
aptly called, is the technique of
fashioning objects from thin metal
wire. An ancient technique in both
Europe and the Americas, it con-
tinued to be used throughout the
Spanish colonial era.

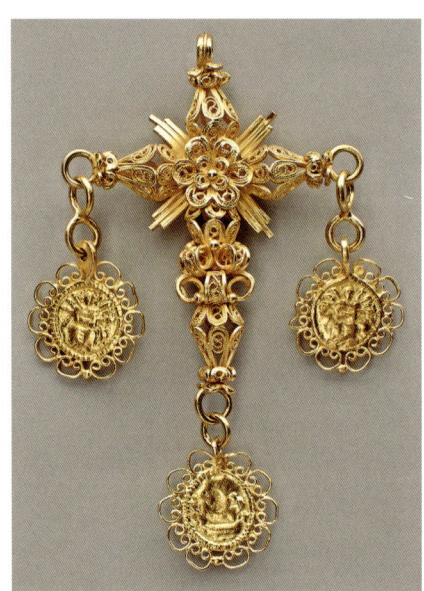

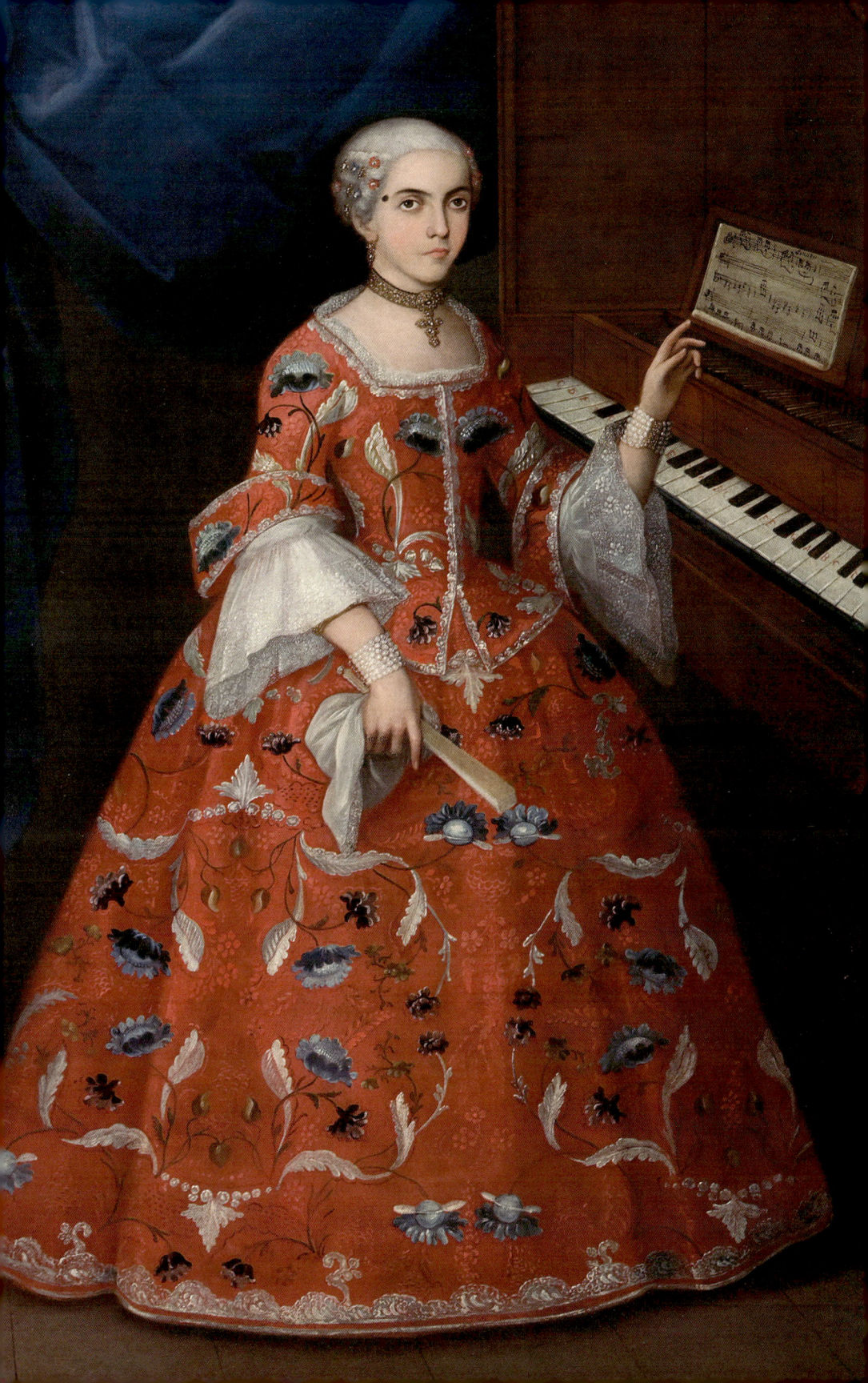

Young Woman with a Harpsichord

Mexico, 1735–50
Oil paint on canvas
61⅝ x 40⅜ in.
Gift of the Collection of
Frederick and Jan Mayer; 2014.209

This young woman, probably a musician or composer from Mexico City, wears a powdered wig and a spectacular red dress of silk brocade, imported either from Asia on the famous Manila galleon ships used in trade across the Pacific, or from Spain, possibly Valencia, known for its luxurious silk production in the eighteenth century.

She wears a gold and diamond choker with crucifix and matching earrings, multiple rings, and two seven-strand pearl bracelets with silver clasps. In her wig are *tembladeras*, flowers attached to springy wires that move with the wearer. She holds a fan, perhaps made of ivory or mother-of-pearl, imported from Europe or Asia, like the ones at right.

Fan

Europe, 1700s
Paint on paper, mother-of-pearl, and gold
9½ in. long
Neusteter Textile Collection: Gift of Mrs. Frances Lowe Scott; 1976.117

Fan

Europe, 1800s
Paint on paper, mother-of-pearl, gold, and silk
10 in. long
Neusteter Textile Collection: Gift of Mrs. Frances Lowe Scott; 1976.125

Fans were extremely popular in colonial Latin America. In 1721 in Santa Fe, New Mexico, the dowry of a young girl named Luisa Luján listed a fan described as "painted ivory from China," while at the opposite end of the Spanish empire in Buenos Aires, Argentina, in 1781, Flora de Azcuenaga's dowry included a fan made of "mother-of-pearl with gold encrustations," similar to the ones here.

These European fans are likely French. The supporting sticks are made of pierced and inlaid mother-of-pearl, while the body is made of painted paper. The open fan at top displays a courting scene bordered by flowers and decorative motifs.

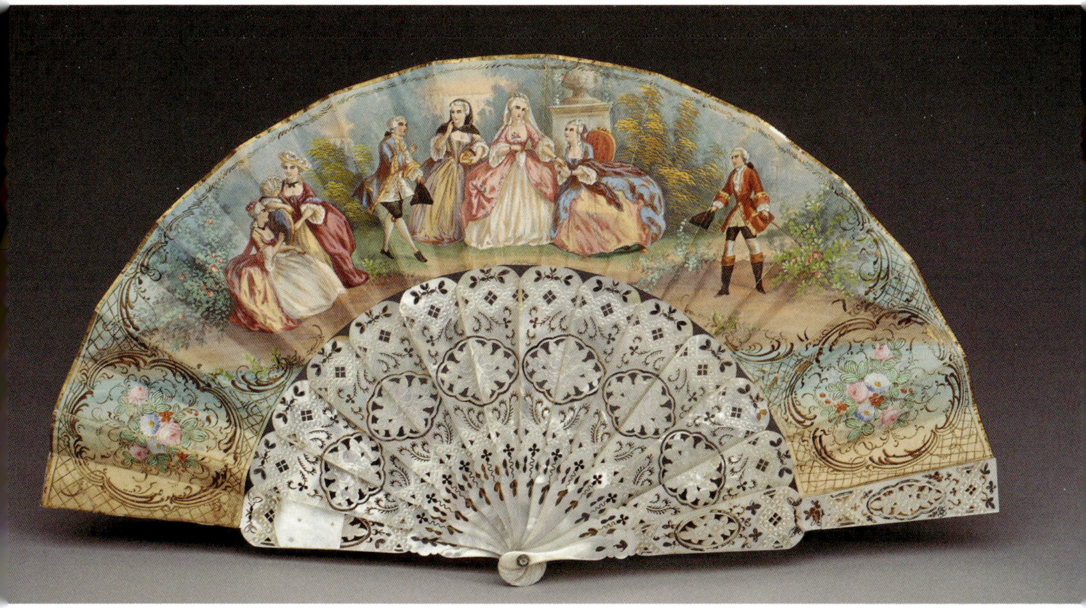

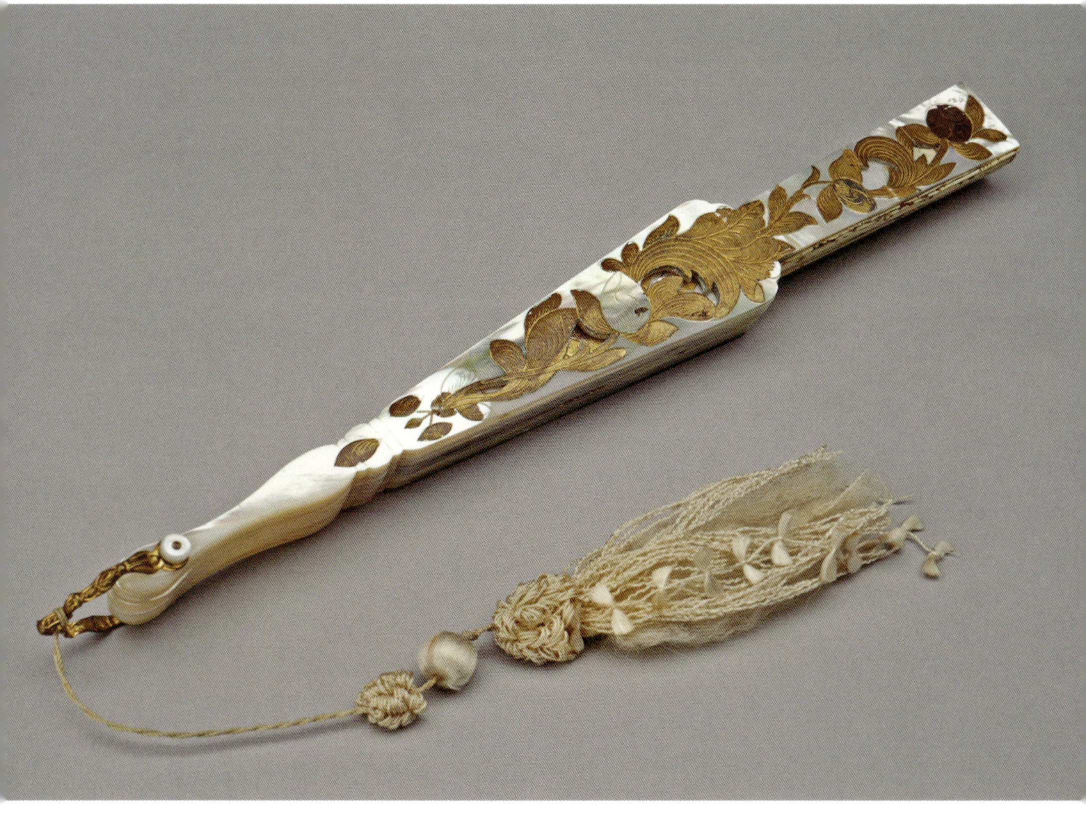

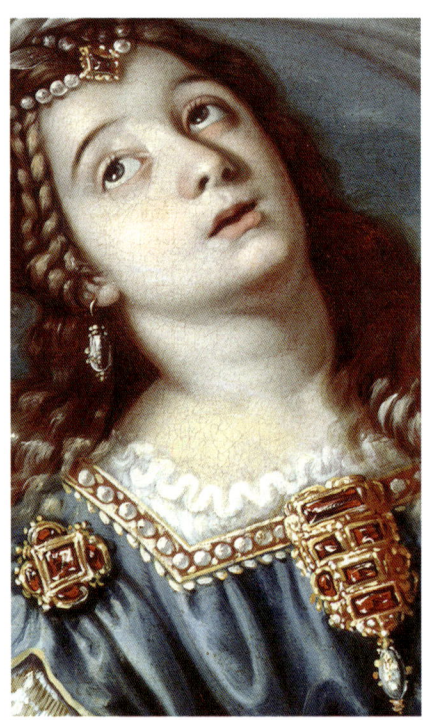

Diego de Borgraf (1618–1686)

Saint Catherine of Alexandria

Puebla, Mexico, 1656
Oil paint on canvas
65¾ x 45¾ in.
Gift of the Collection of Frederick
and Jan Mayer; 2011.426

In colonial Latin America, paintings often show saints and the Virgin Mary decked out in elaborate period jewelry. Here Saint Catherine is painted as an upper-class woman wearing sumptuous fabrics, silver and gold pendant earrings, and an elaborate ruby and pearl headband. Large gold and ruby brooches adorn her chest and shoulders. The precious stones are painted with small dabs of brilliantly colored paint and dotted with highlights of white, gold, and silver.

Saint Catherine of Alexandria (Egypt) was imprisoned and martyred for converting Romans to Christianity during the third century. The artist, Diego de Borgraf, was born in Antwerp but worked as a Spanish court painter during the time of Diego Velázquez before immigrating to Puebla, Mexico, with Bishop Juan de Palafox y Mendoza in 1640.

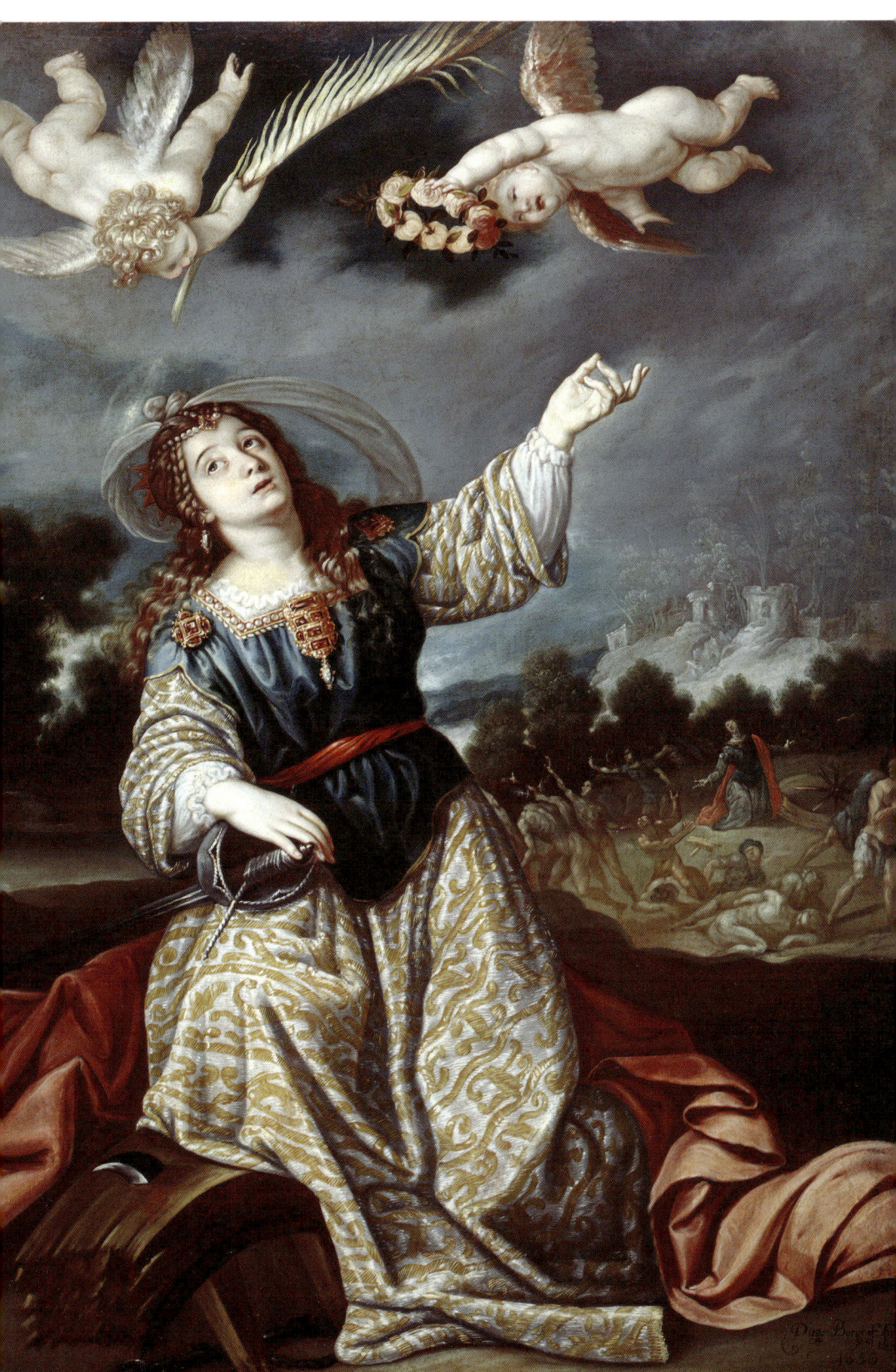

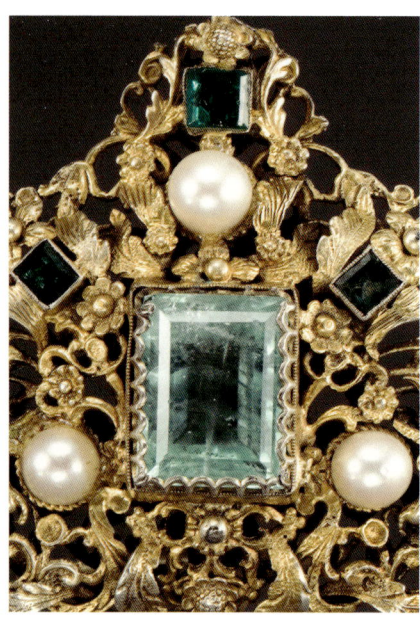

(opposite, top, and detail left)

Tiara

Colombia or Ecuador, 1690–1750
Gilt silver, emeralds, and pearls
2½ x 5½ x 3¾ in.
Gift of Robert J. Stroessner; 1992.74

Tiaras and other forms of hair ornament were common among women of all classes in colonial Latin America. Upper-class women often wore elaborate ones encrusted with jewels, as seen in portraits and as described in documents.

For example, in 1781 in Buenos Aires, Argentina, sixteen-year-old Flora de Azcuenaga had a tiara "made of silver and gold … with a leaf and flower motif. In the center was a bird placed on a gold trunk and covered with 135 rose-colored diamonds, with an almond-shaped diamond hanging from its beak and a ruby eye."

(opposite, bottom)

Tiara

Colombia or Ecuador, 1850–80
Gilt copper
2¼ x 5¼ x 5½ in.
Gift of the Stapleton Foundation of Latin American Colonial Art, made possible by the Renchard family; 1990.581

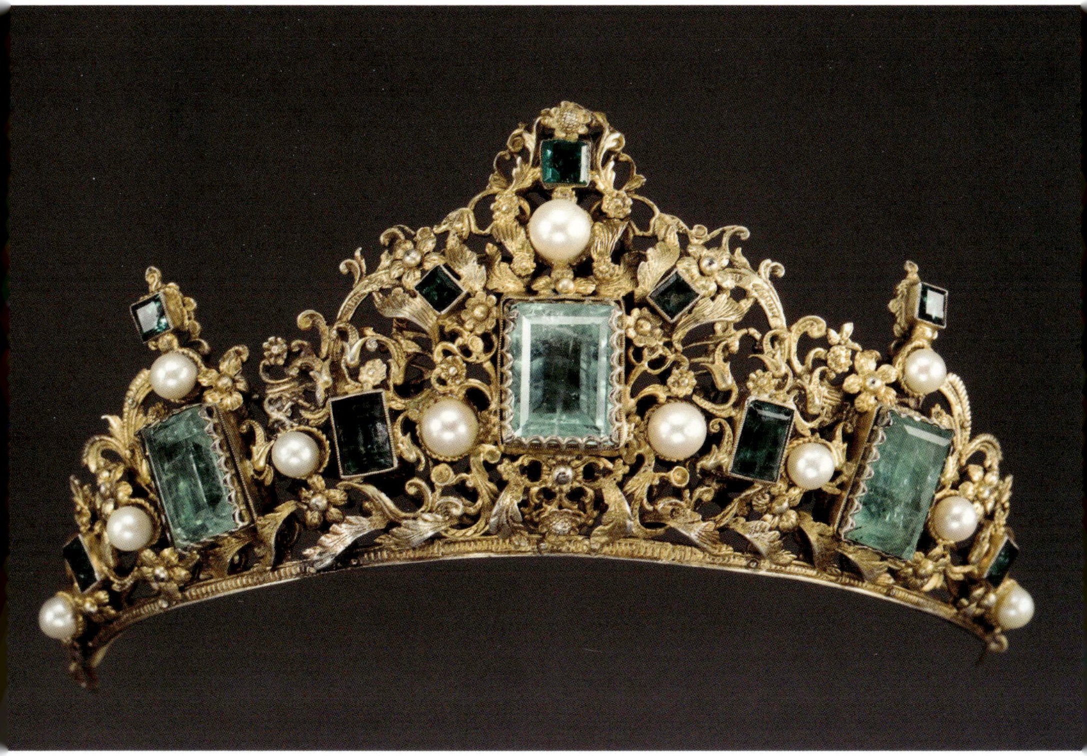

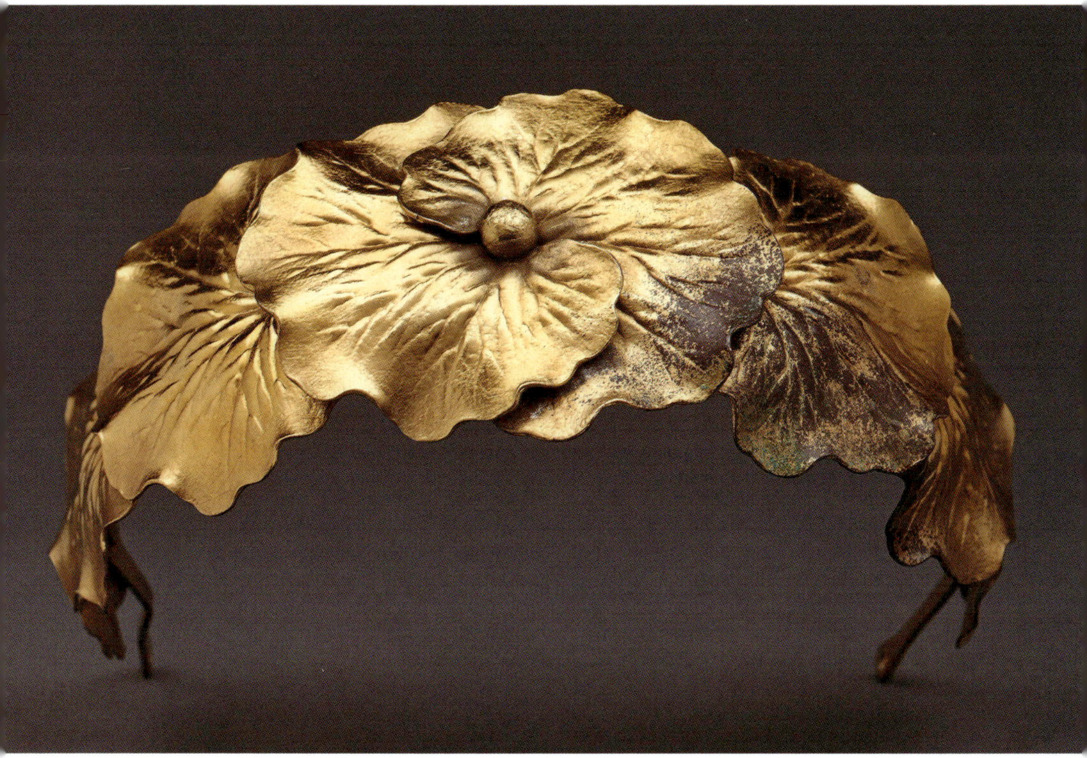

Portraits and Jewelry

Both men and women are excessive in their apparel. Precious stones and pearls further much their vain ostentation.

—Thomas Gage, an English Dominican friar traveling in Mexico and Guatemala, 1625–37

Portraiture became increasingly important in colonial Latin America, where local artists generally followed the accepted canons for official portraiture in Europe. However, in the Americas the focus on social standing often took precedence over conveying the personality of the subject. Artists focused their attention on depicting rich details of luxurious clothing, jewelry, and objects that alluded to the subject's wealth, status, abilities, and accomplishments.

Women are painted adorned with tiaras or hair ornaments, opulent necklaces with pendants and matching earrings, and multiple rings and bracelets. Men proudly display gold buttons and braids, hat ornaments, badges of military office, insignias of religious confraternities, rings, watch fobs, and chatelaines with small tools similar to the modern Swiss Army knife. Coats-of-arms or cartouches with inscriptions outlining the sitter's heritage, accomplishments, and honors are often included in portraits of the era.

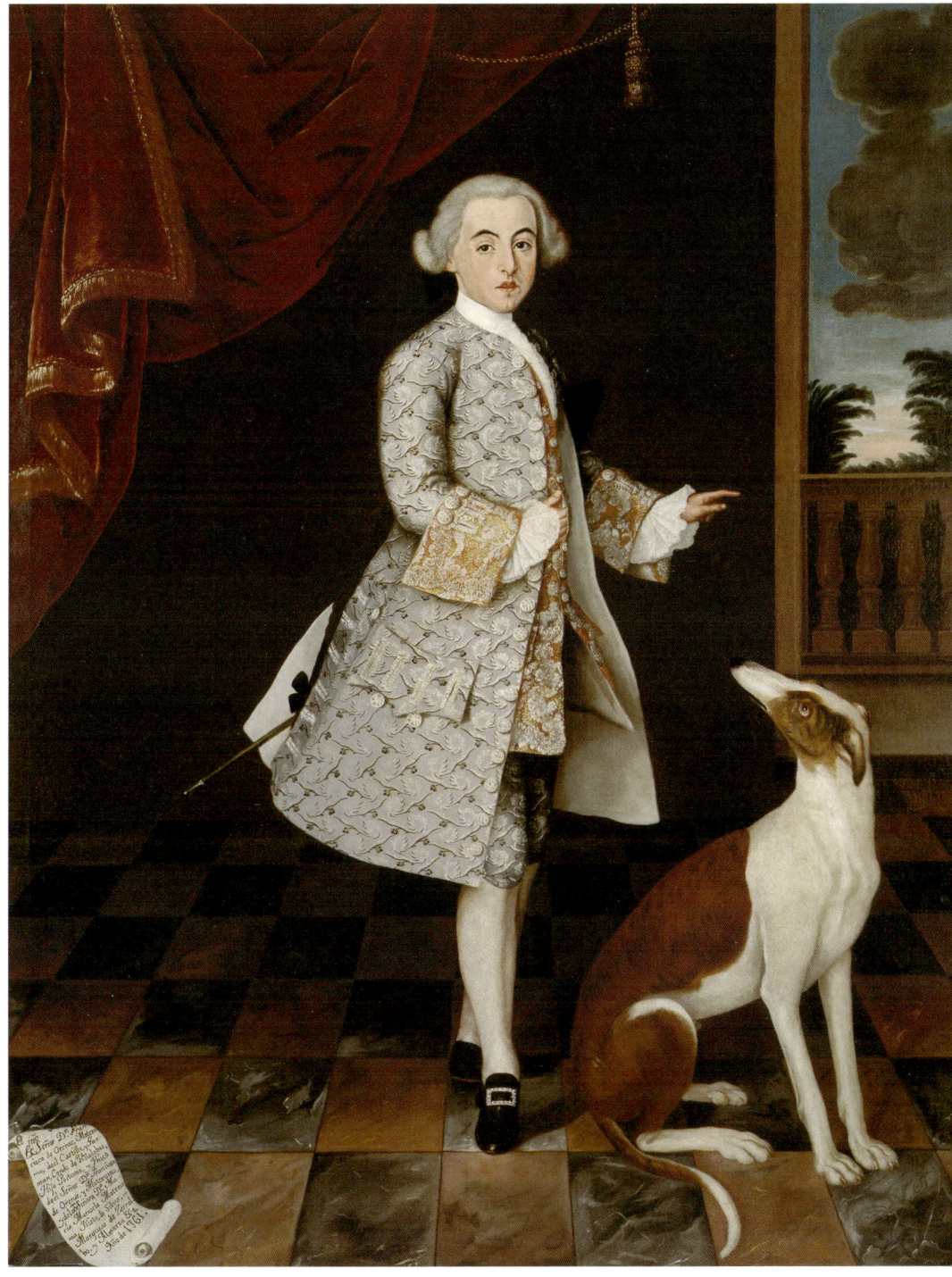

Portrait of Francisco de Orense y Moctezuma, Count of Villalobos

Mexico, 1761
Oil paint on canvas
74 x 59 in.
Gift of the Collection of Frederick
and Jan Mayer; 2011.427

This young man is wearing luxurious clothing woven from silver
and gold thread (literally, silk thread
wrapped with tiny ribbons of real
gold and silver), silver buttons, and
diamond shoe buckles. Underneath
his short, powdered wig, a long
braid tied with a black ribbon
hangs down his back, and a sword
protrudes backward from under his
coat.

During the early days of the
Spanish arrival in Mexico, prior
to hostilities, Moctezuma married
several of his daughters and nieces
to Spaniards, including Hernán
Cortés and many of his officers.
Throughout the colonial period,
their descendants, such as this
young man, proudly claimed their
Aztec nobility, as noted in the inscription at lower left (detail below).

Ramón de Torres (active 1775–1800)

Portrait of Don Estéban de la Carrera y Prado

Mexico, 1782
Oil paint on canvas
38 x 32 in.
Collection of Frederick and Jan Mayer;
17.2014

We can tell by the red Greek cross
with fleurs-de-lis ends pinned or
sewn to his jacket that this gentleman
was a member of the religious-
military Order of Calatrava. The
cross also appears on a jeweled
pendant suspended from an eagle
pin on his jacket. Similar insignia
pendants can be seen on page 36.

Silver-thread embroidery and
silver buttons adorn his uniform,
and silver and red silk tassels peek
out from underneath his vest. A tri-
corn hat, sword, and walking stick
appear at his right side.

A native of Galicia, Spain,
Carrera had an illustrious career in
the New World as Commissioner
of War and Royal Treasurer of the
Port of Acapulco.

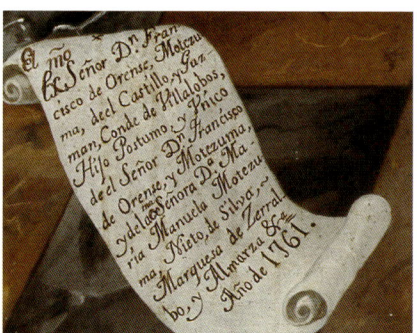

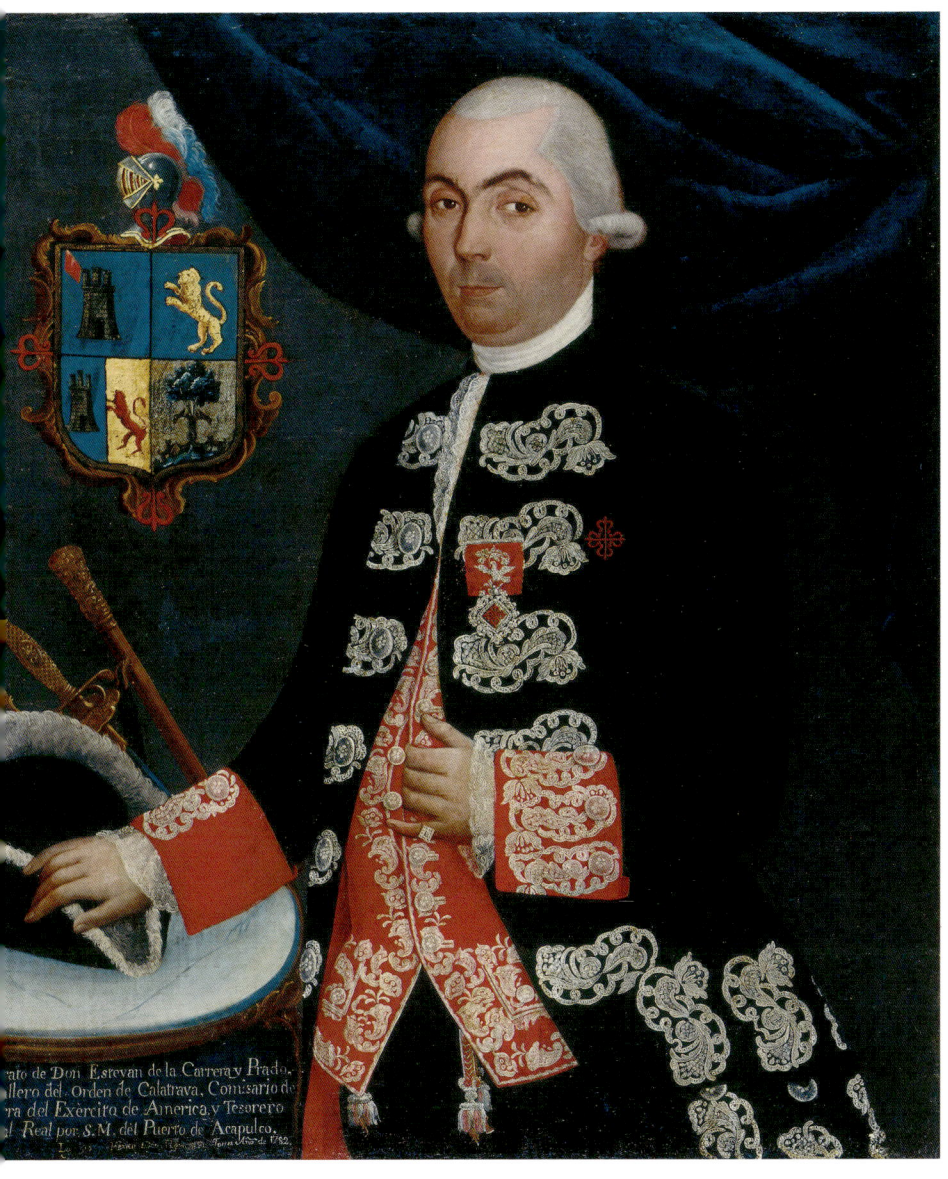

rato de Don Estevan de la Carrera y Prado,
llero del Orden de Calatrava, Comisario de
ra del Exército de America, y Tesorero
l Real por S.M. del Puerto de Acapulco.

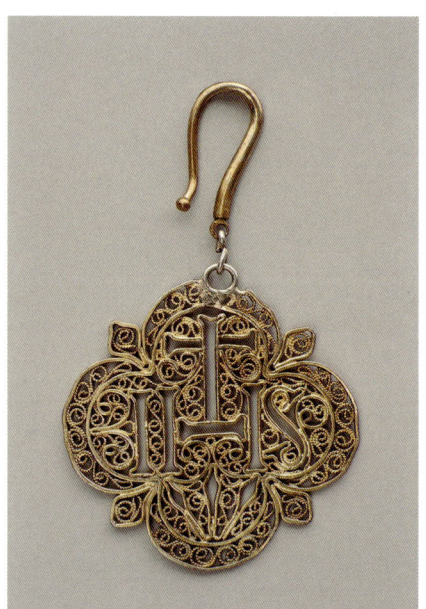

Insignia Medallion

Colombia or Ecuador, 1800s
Gold filigree and cast gold
Gift of the Stapleton Foundation of
Latin American Colonial Art, made
possible by the Renchard family;
1990.537

Insignia medallions were popular
among both men and women in
the colonial era. Women often
wore them suspended from choker
necklaces; men wore them hanging
from pins on their chests, much like
military medals today.

This filigree medallion bears
the IHS monogram (the first three
letters of Christ's name in Greek),
a symbol often associated with the
Jesuit order.

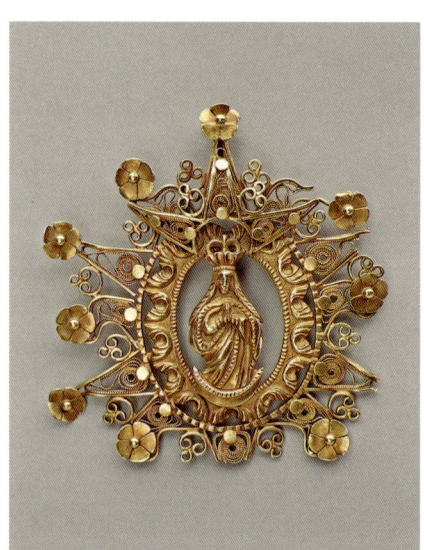

(middle left)

Medallion with Virgin Mary

Colombia or Ecuador, 1800s
Gilt-silver filigree
2½ in. diameter
Gift of the Stapleton Foundation of
Latin American Colonial Art, made
possible by the Renchard family;
1990.625

This filigree medallion indicates
that the person who wore it was
probably a member of a lay organi-
zation dedicated to the Immaculate
Conception of the Virgin Mary,
shown in the center.

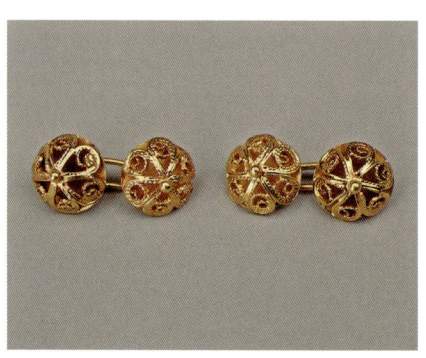

(opposite, bottom left)

Buttons or Cuff Links

Colombia or Ecuador, 1800s
Gold filigree
¼ in. diameter (each)
Gift of the Stapleton Foundation of
Latin American Colonial Art, made
possible by the Renchard family;
1990.612a, b

Prior to the 1800s, fancy buttons
were usually not sewn onto clothing, but were fashioned like cuff
links so they could be transferred
from one garment to another.

(right)

Strike-a-light

Peru or Bolivia, 1700s
Silver and iron
12⅛ x 2⅝ in.
Bequest of Robert J. Stroessner;
1992.73

Tobacco was a New World product,
unknown in Europe before contact
with the Americas. The smoking of
tobacco became extremely popular in Europe and the colonies.
Elaborate tools evolved for using
tobacco such as tobacco holders,
snuff boxes, and portable strike-a-
lights, such as this one.

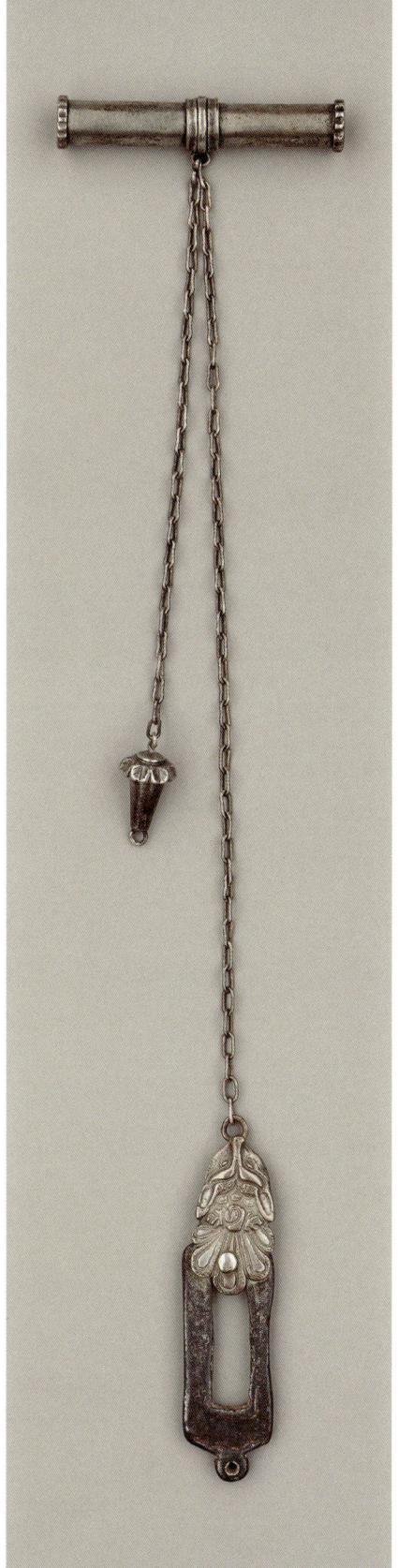

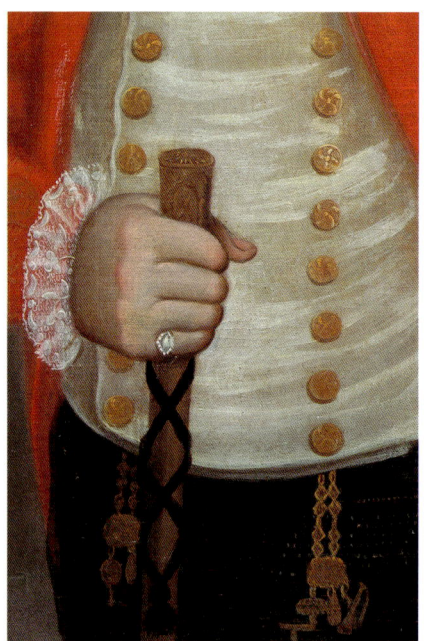

(opposite, and detail left)

Francisco Aguirre

Portrait of Francisco Javier Paredes

Mexico, about 1800
Oil paint on canvas
40½ x 31¼ in.
Collection of Frederick and Jan Mayer;
14.2014

This gentleman wears a diamond pinky ring, gold buttons on his vest, a sword, and two chatelaines (hanging waist ornaments). An elaborate chained medal is pinned to his hat, and he holds a walking stick. Francisco Javier Paredes was a native of Asturias, Spain, and served as a colonel in the Spanish army in Mexico.

(left)

Hat or Waist Ornament

Mexico, early 1800s
Gold and diamond
5 x 1⅛ in.
Gift of Robert J. Stroessner; 1991.1137

The insignia piece at the bottom of this ornament shows an eagle and a snake flanking a small diamond. This object may have served as part of a chatelaine or as a hat ornament, as seen in the portrait at right.

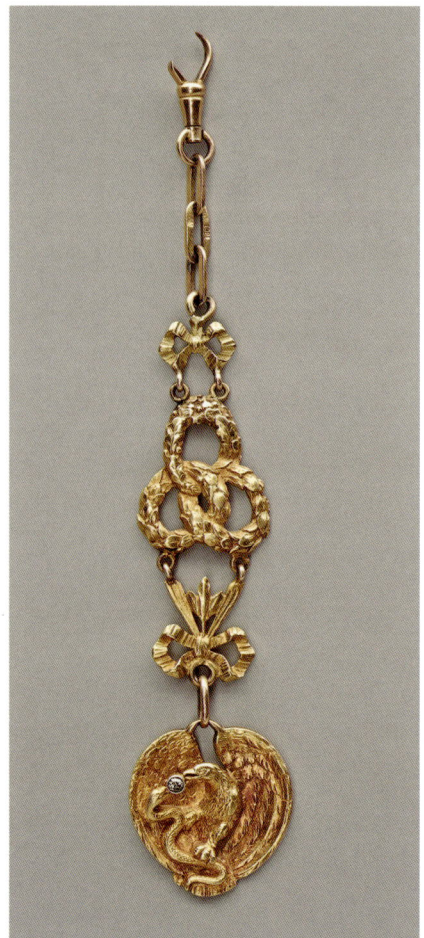

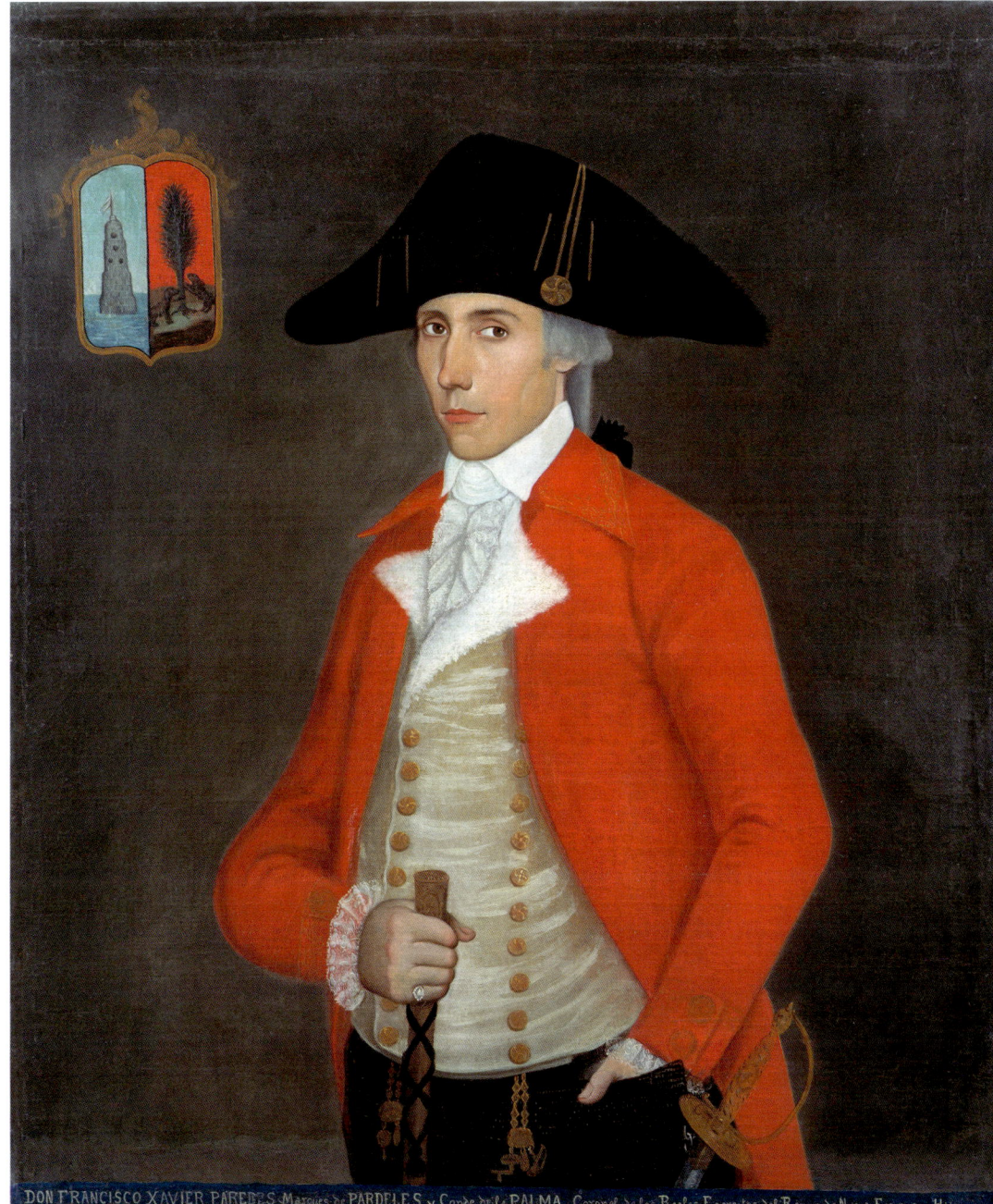

DON FRANCISCO XAVIER PAREDES Marques de PARDELES y Conde de la PALMA Coronel de los Reales Egercitos del Reyno de Nueva España; Hijo
Legitimo de D. Juan Fran.co Paredes y de D.ª Anna Fernandez Rachel Gamoneda; Nacio en Luarca en el Conz.º de Valdes Principado de Asturias Obispado de Oviedo
en 11 de Mayo de 1758, de hedad de 29 años.

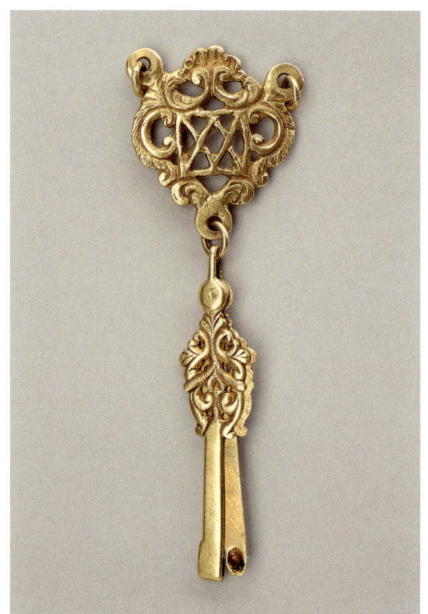

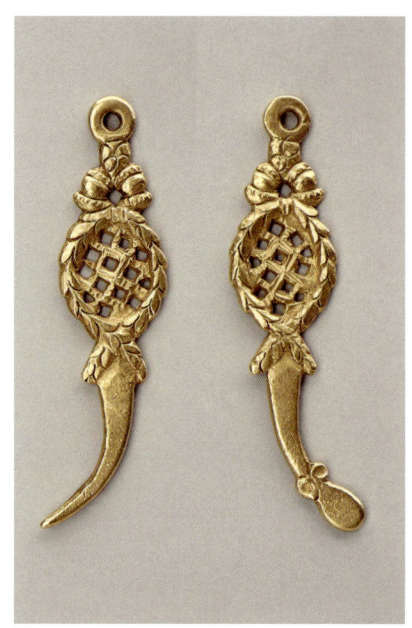

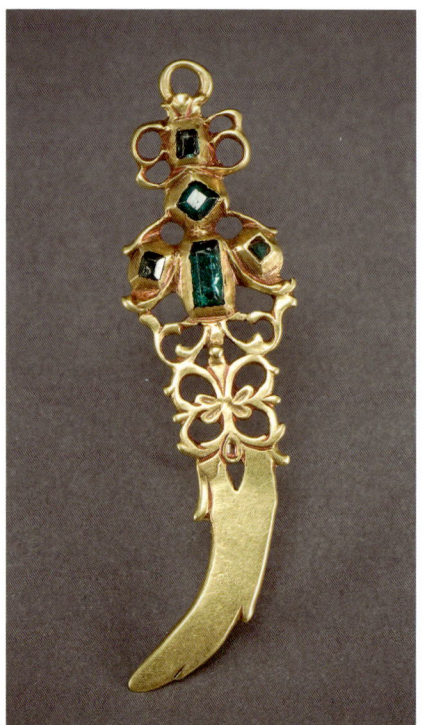

(clockwise from bottom left)

Chatelaine Tools

Colombia or Ecuador
Gold and emeralds, 1650s, 2½ x ½ in.
Gold, 1600s, 3¼ x 1 in.
Gold, 1700s, 2 x ½ in. (each)
Gifts of the Stapleton Foundation of
Latin American Colonial Art, made
possible by the Renchard family;
1990.525, 1990.623, 1990.761, 1990.618

Chatelaines originated in Europe as
a means of attaching a watch or key
to one's belt. Over time the form
evolved to include useful miniature
tools and implements such as scis-
sors, pencils, toothpicks, grooming
tools, and folding knives—the
colonial equivalent to the modern-
day Swiss Army knife, as seen in
the portraits at right and on the
previous page.

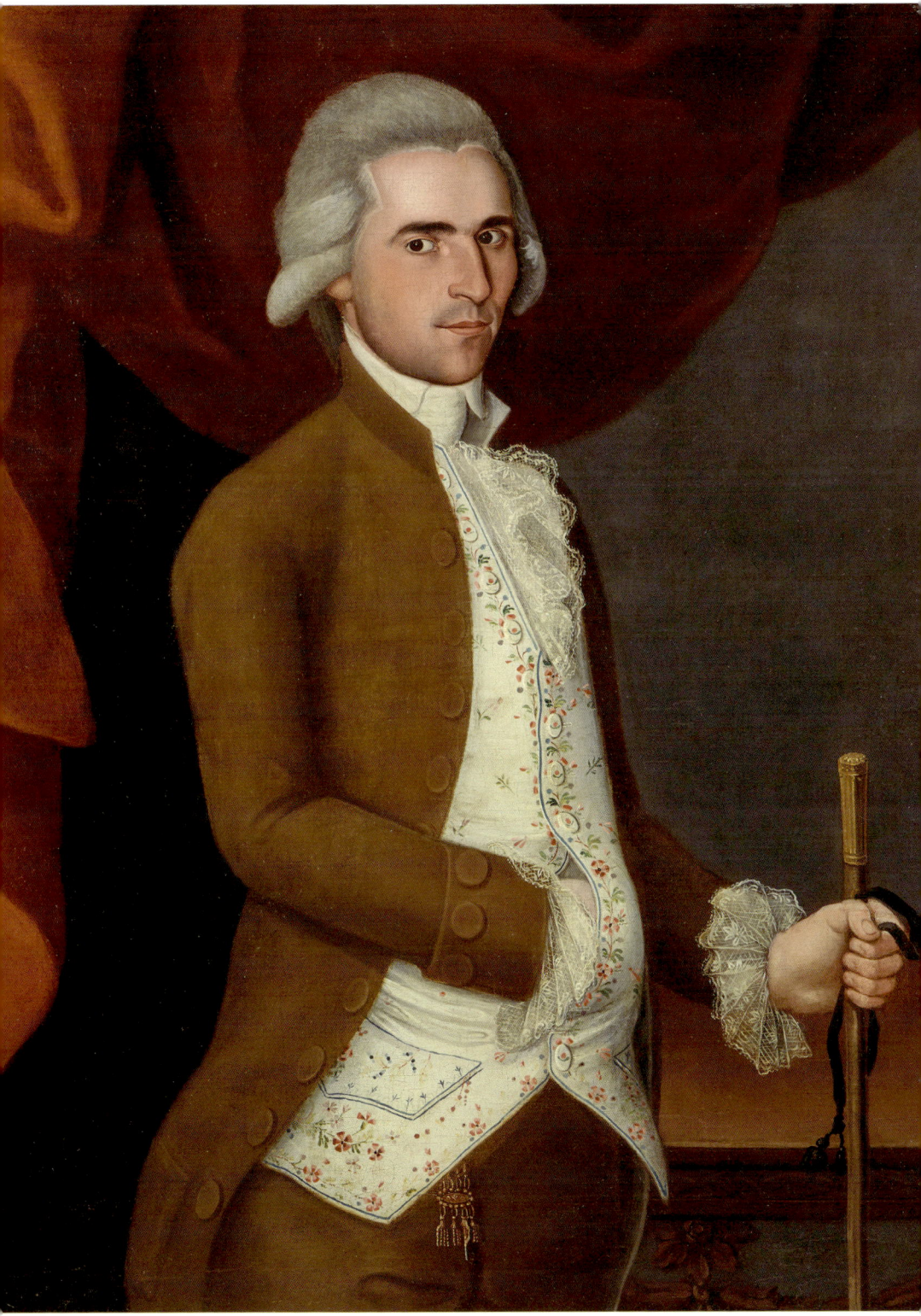

(previous page)

Attributed to
José Joaquín Esquivel

Portrait of a Gentleman

Mexico, late 1700s
Oil paint on canvas
34½ x 27⅓ in.
Collection of Frederick and Jan Mayer;
15.2014

This gentleman wears late colonial period dress. His subdued yet elegant jacket and embroidered silk vest are accented with lace. In his left hand he holds a gold-tipped cane. A chatelaine (hanging waist ornament) peeks out from under the lower edge of his vest.

(opposite)

Portrait of Bernardo de Gálvez

Mexico, after 1779
Oil paint on canvas; gilt wood frame
28¾ x 18½ in.
Gift of the Collection of Frederick and Jan Mayer; 2013.327

This painting is mounted as a scroll so it could be rolled up for travel. It depicts Bernardo de Gálvez wearing a military uniform with gold epaulets and buttons. We can tell from his jewelry that he was a member of two prestigious religious-military orders in Spain. A red foliated cross in the shape of a dagger, the insignia of the knightly order of Santiago, appears on a pin or patch and on a matching pendant suspended from a diamond bow pin. His belt buckle bears the royal insignia of the Order of Carlos III, King of Spain (ruled 1759–88), to which he was appointed in 1779. Other insignia jewelry can be seen on page 36.

Several members of the Gálvez family served the Spanish crown as government officials in the Americas. They contributed funds and troops to the U.S. independence movement. Galveston Bay and Galveston, Texas, are named for Bernardo, who served as the Spanish governor of New Orleans from 1777 to 1783 and defeated the British forces at Baton Rouge, Louisiana; Mobile, Alabama; Pensacola, Florida; and the Bahamas. He later served as Viceroy of Mexico.

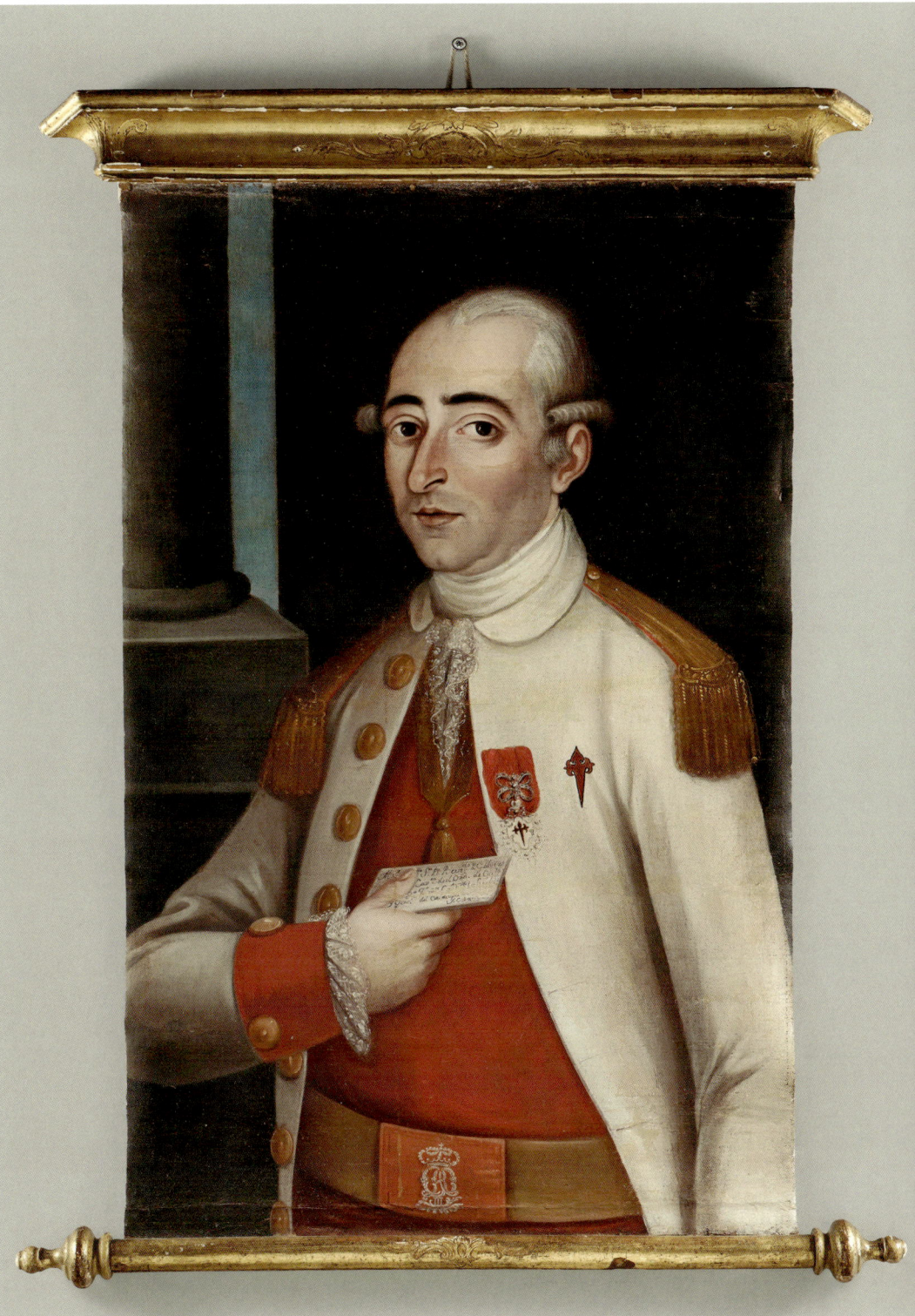

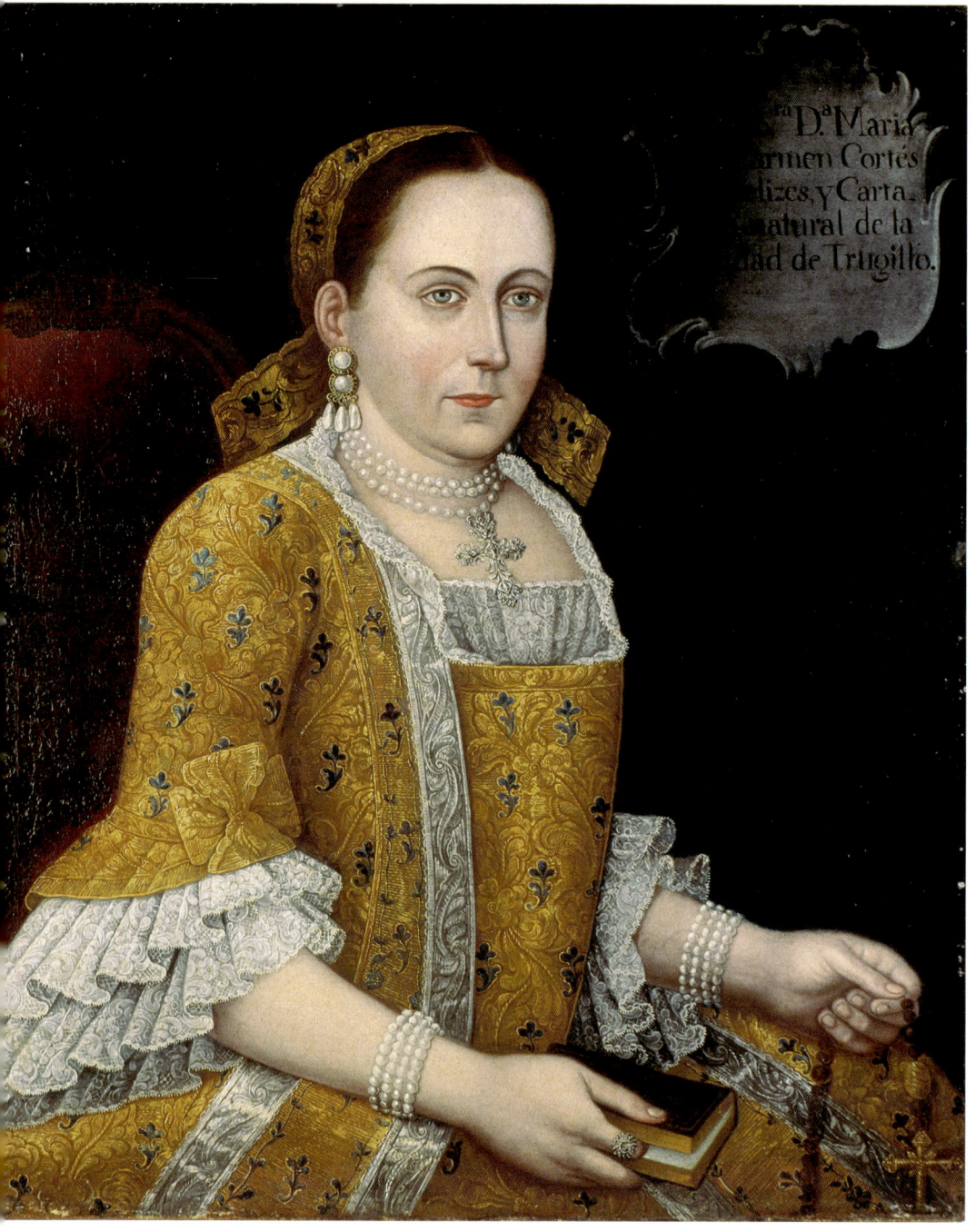

Sra. Dª Maria
[...]rmen Cortes
[...]lizes, y Carta[...]
[...]natural de la
[...]ad de Truçillo.

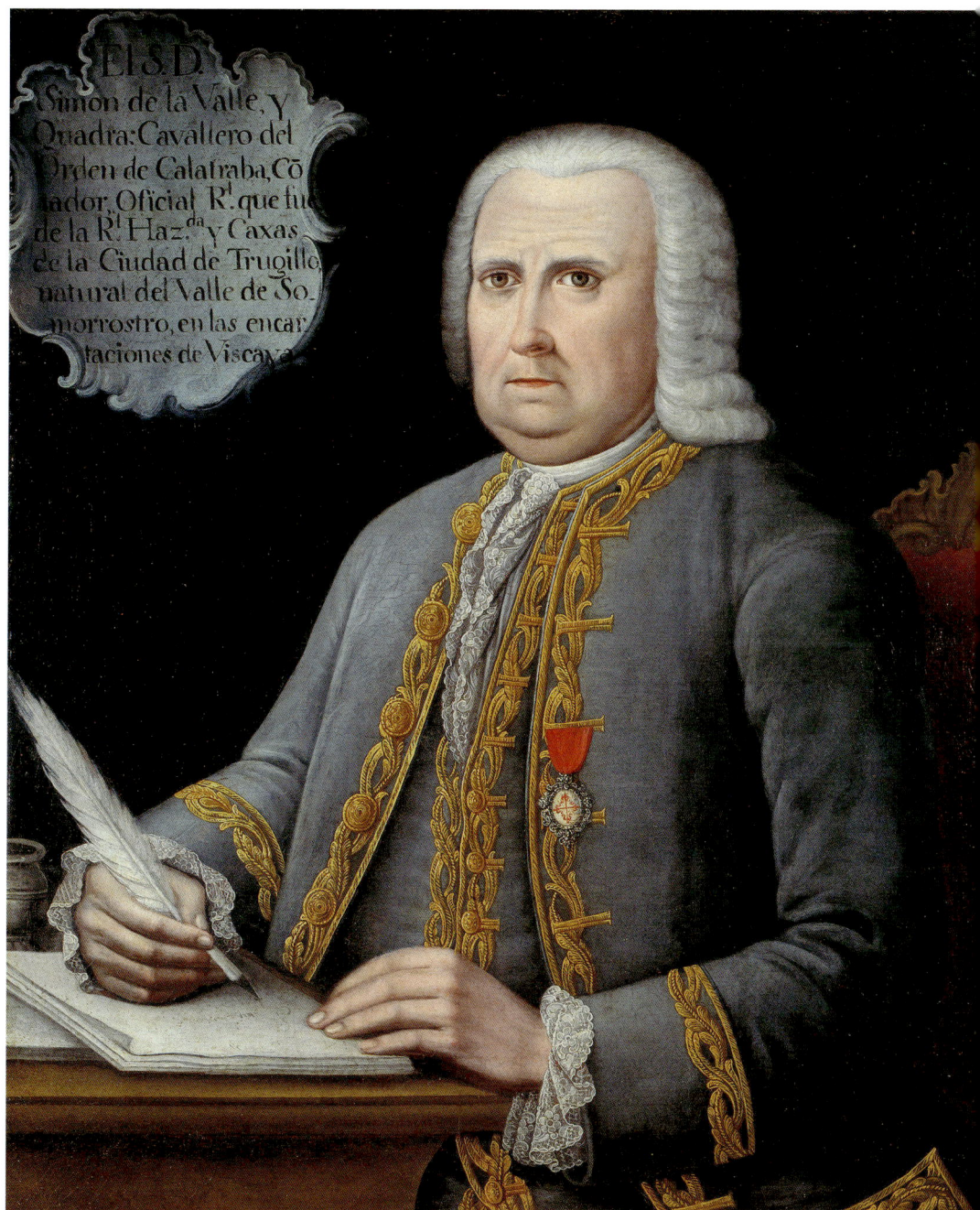

El S.r D.n
Simon de la Valle, y
Quadra: Cavallero del
Orden de Calatraba, Cõ
tador, Oficial R.l que fue
de la R.l Haz.da y Caxas
de la Ciudad de Trugillo,
natural del Valle de So_
morrostro, en las encar_
taciones de Viscaya

Portrait of María del Carmen Cortés Santelizes y Cartavio

Portrait of Simón de la Valle y Cuadra

Peru, about 1760
Oil paint on canvas
30½ x 25 in. (each)
Funds from Frederick and Jan Mayer, Carl and Marilynn Thoma, Jim and Marybeth Vogelzang, and Harley and Lorraine Higbie; 2000.250.1, .2

Simón de la Valle was made a Knight of the Spanish Order of Calatrava in 1750. In his portrait he proudly wears the red equilateral cross insignia of this prestigious order hanging from a red ribbon on his velvet coat trimmed with gold thread.

His wife is shown in the portrait at left. She wears a brocade dress made with gold and silk thread and adorned with silver-thread trim. Her elaborate jewelry includes pearl chandelier earrings, a three-strand pearl necklace with a suspended cross of silver and diamonds, pearl bracelets, a diamond ring, and a rosary with a gold filigree cross.

Juan de Sáenz
(active 1780–1815)

Portrait of Fernando de Musitu Zalvide

Mexico, about 1800
Oil paint on canvas
64¾ x 36 in.
Purchased in memory of Frederick Mayer with funds from Lorraine and Harley Higbie, Marilynn and Carl Thoma, Patrick Pierce, Alianza de las Artes Americanas, and department acquisition funds; 2008.27

With the rise of the merchant class in the late 1700s came the early stages of the independence movement in Latin America. Likewise, a shift in portrait painting began to occur—a movement away from portraying nobility and status toward emphasizing realism and capturing the likeness of an individual, as is evident in this picture of a young man from one of the wealthiest families in Mexico.

Although no other signs of wealth are present, this gentleman wears diamond shoe buckles, a common form of jewelry for both men and women. They could be transferred from one pair of shoes to another. He also wears two hanging tassels that could suspend watches or disguise chatelaines.

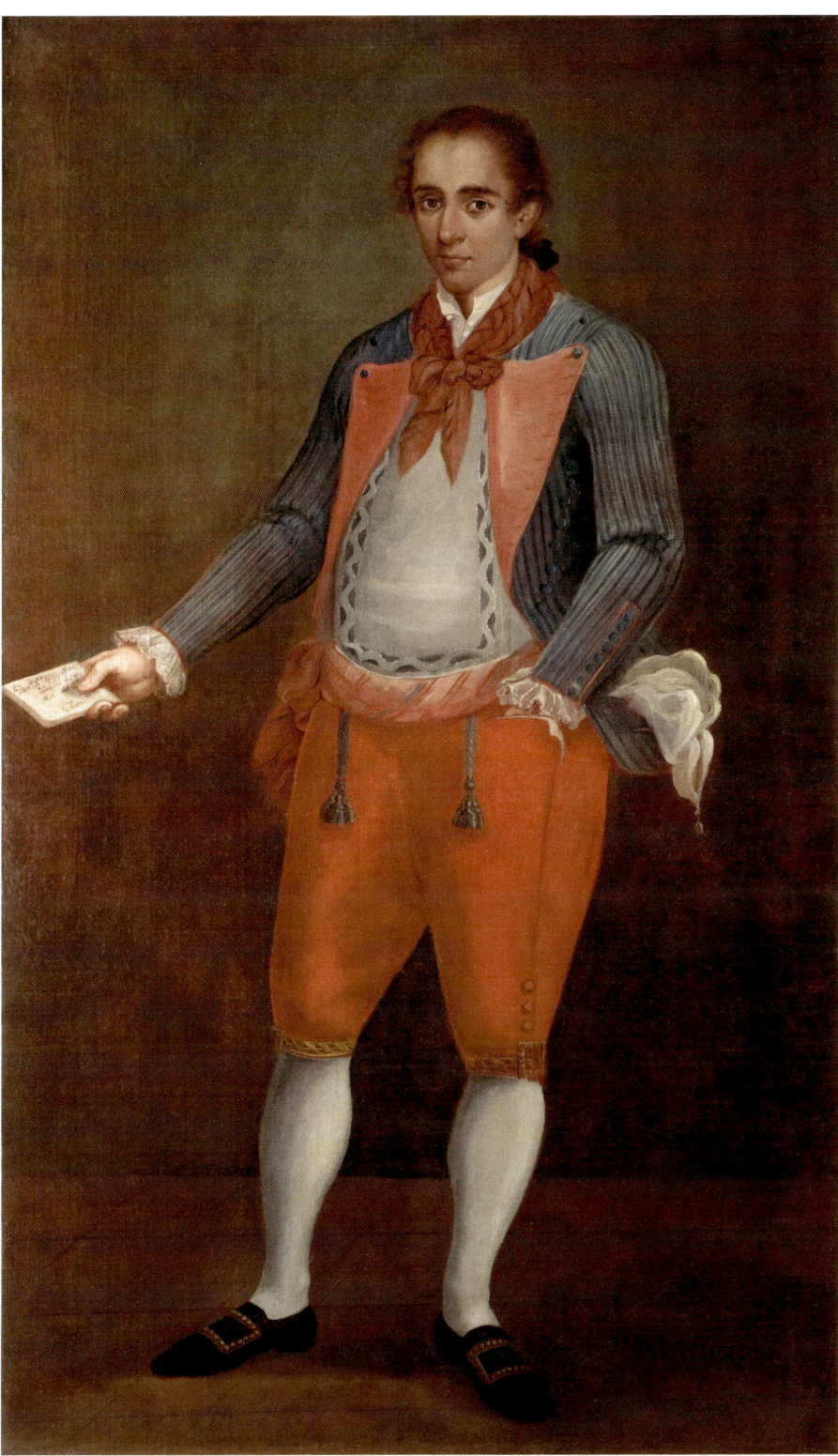

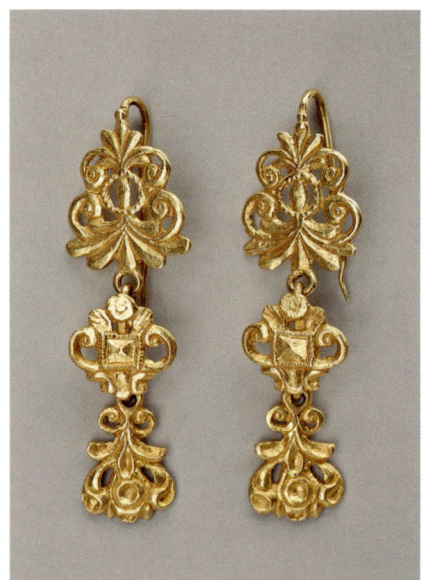

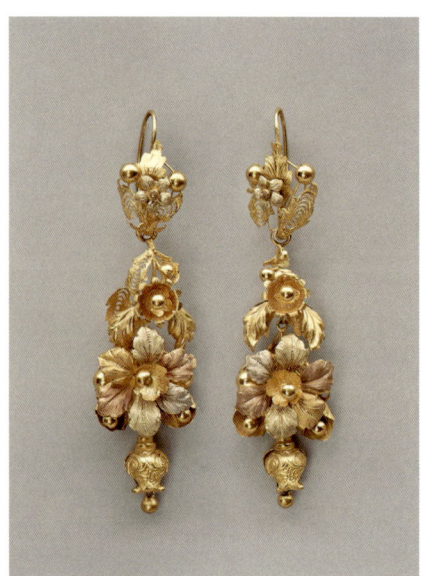

(left)

Two Pairs of Earrings

Colombia or Ecuador, 1800s
Gold
2¼ x ½ in., 2 x ½ in.
Gift of the Stapleton Foundation of
Latin American Colonial Art, made
possible by the Renchard family;
1990.616a, b and 1990.620a, b

Linked in three sections, the earrings
at left are crafted to form fleurs-
de-lis and faceted jewel-like forms.
The reversible earrings at bottom
left are made using yellow and rose
gold to create floral motifs on one
side and shell forms on the other.

(opposite)

Woman with an Earring

Bogotá, Colombia, about 1850
Oil paint on canvas
31½ x 24¼ in.
Gift of Dr. Belinda Straight; 1984.718

While colonial portraits aimed to
show the status of the sitter rather
than a physical likeness, a focus
on realism and individual identity
emerged in the early 1800s with
the independence movement in
Latin America. This post-colonial
artist painted a highly individualized
portrait that captures the essence
of this elderly woman. Although
the prominent gold and pearl drop
earring hints at her wealth, this
stand-out element also contributes
to the woman's confident—almost
defiant—attitude.

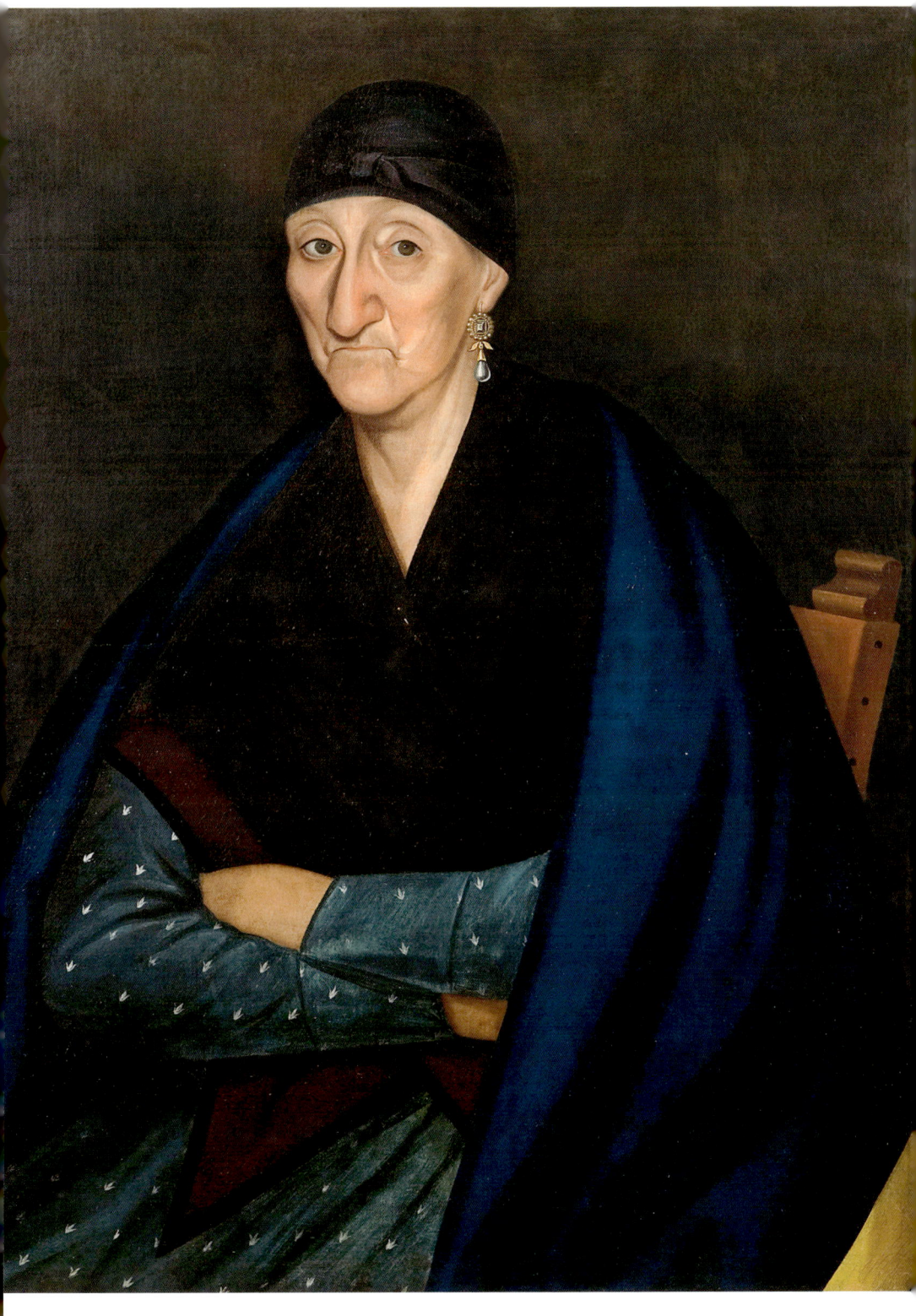

Jewelry Boxes

No Mexican lady, married or single, has yet paid me a morning visit without diamonds.
        —Fanny Calderón de la Barca,
          a Scottish visitor to Mexico,
            1839—42

Chests with drawers were used to store jewelry. One with seven drawers was described in 1661 in Bogotá, Colombia, as holding a necklace of twenty-four gold beads with an image of the Virgin Mary with three pendant pearls and a matching bracelet; a gold image of the Christ Child with two pearls hanging from his arms; several gold chains; three pearl choker necklaces, one with a cross in the middle; bracelets of coral and pearls; and two brooches, four rings, and several sets of gold earrings set with emeralds, pearls, purple stones, and white crystal.

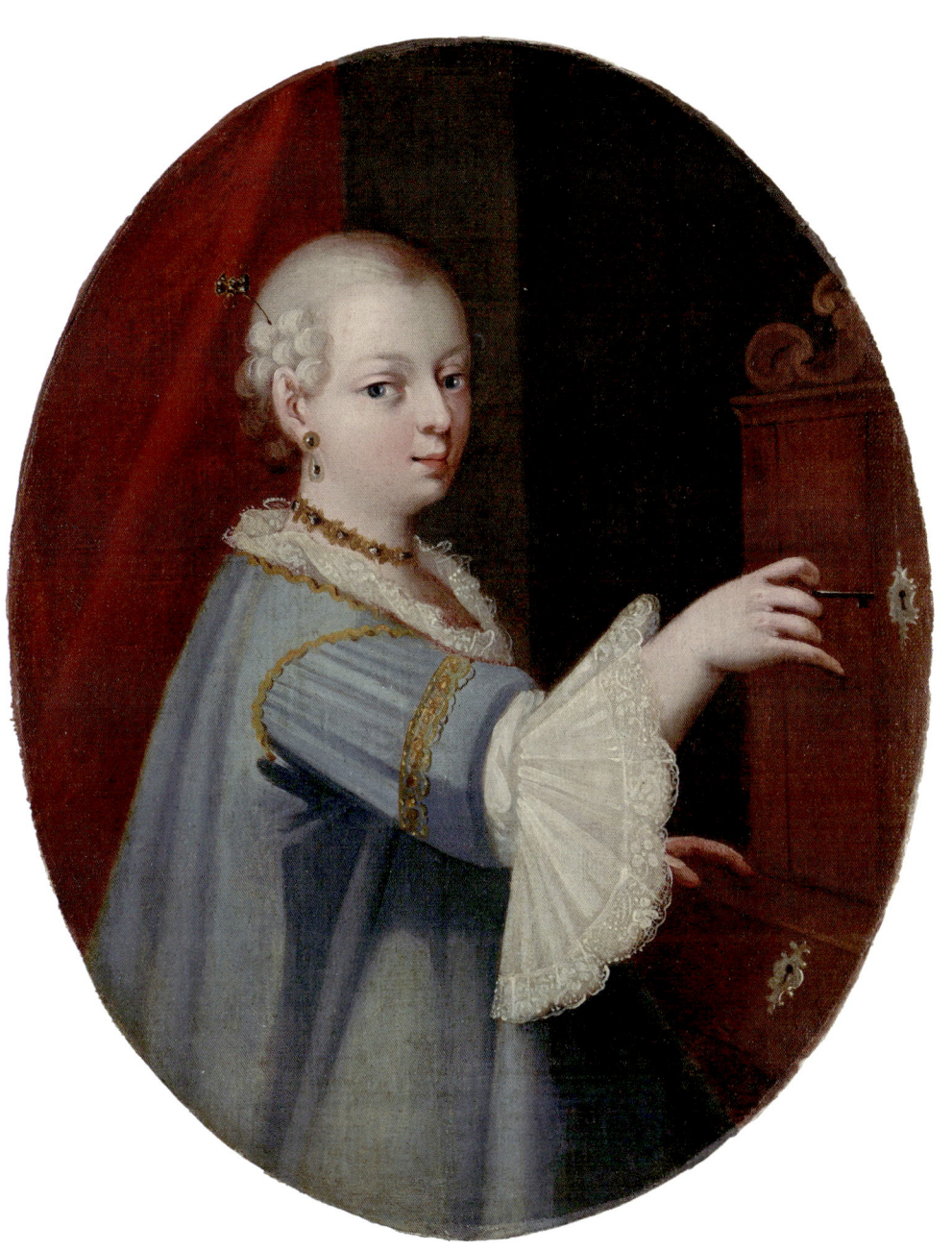

Lady Locking her Jewelry Cabinet

Mexico, mid 1700s
Oil paint on canvas
21¾ x 16½ in.
Lent by David and Boo Butler; 13.2014

This well-to-do young woman has just adorned herself with elegant drop earrings, a gold choker necklace, and a type of hair ornament known as a *tembladera*, with a jeweled butterfly or honeybee mounted on a spiral wire so that it flutters as she moves her head.

Cabinet with Drawers

Ecuador or Europe, 1700s
Wood with ivory and metal inlay
11½ x 21¾ x 9¾ in.
Gift of the Stapleton Foundation of Latin American Colonial Art, made possible by the Renchard family; 1990.314

Lock-boxes such as this were often used to store luxury goods and jewelry. The inlaid ivory plaques are incised with black, and several depict scenes from the Labors of Hercules, the mythical founder of Spain.

Jewelry or Trinket Chest

Mexico or New Mexico, about 1800
Painted glass with gold leaf, and tin-coated iron
6⅛ x 7⅝ x 5⅝ in.
Purchased in memory of Ann Casey Ammons by Alianza de las Artes Americanas and Las Malinches; 2010.439

Spain served as one of only two major sources of tin in Europe, and objects made from metal (either copper or iron) coated with tin have been popular among Spanish and Spanish colonial artists for centuries. The tradition continues in Spain, Mexico, and the U.S. Southwest today. This small chest is decorated with reverse glass painting and likely was used to store jewelry or small valuable objects.

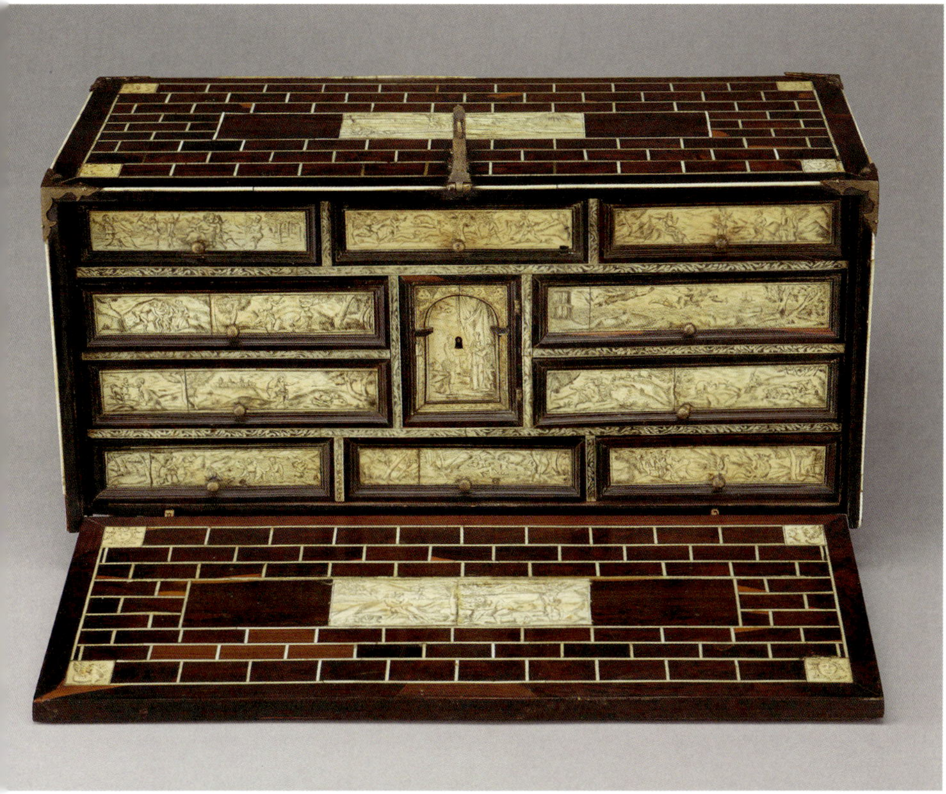

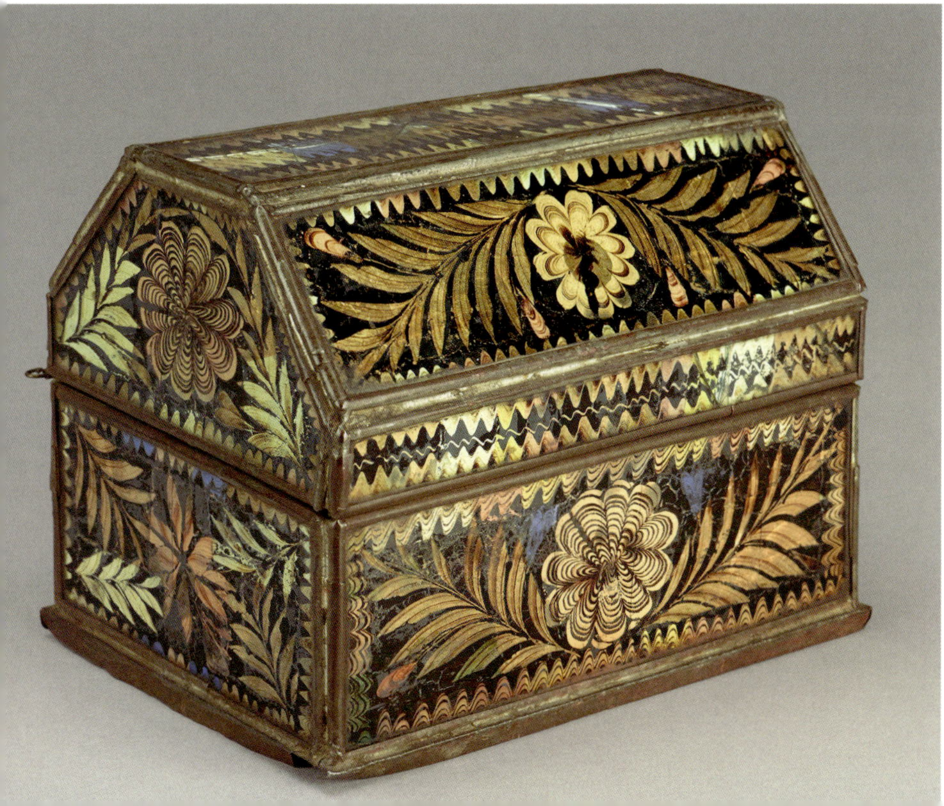

(opposite, top)

Chest with Drawers and Mirror

Colombia, 1700s
Wood, silver, *barniz de pasto*, silver leaf, glass, and bone
7½ x 13½ x 11½ in.
Gift of the Stapleton Foundation of Latin American Colonial Art, made possible by the Renchard family; 1990.301

This chest, likely used to store jewelry and other luxury goods, was decorated with a pre-Hispanic technique known as *barniz de pasto*. The artist would chew the resin of the Andean mopa-mopa shrub, spit it out and add pigment, and then stretch the substance into a thin sheet that could be applied to wood using heated stones. During the colonial period, silver leaf was added to enhance luminosity.

Chests with drawers were used to store jewelry such as one described in Bogotá, Colombia, in 1661, with seven drawers full of gold, pearl, emerald, and coral jewelry.

(opposite, bottom)

Chest with Animal Scenes

Colombia, 1700s
Wood, silver, *barniz de pasto*, and silver leaf
15¼ x 22½ x 10¼ in.
Collection of Frederick and Jan Mayer; 5.2011

Like the chest with drawers, this large chest was decorated with a pre-Hispanic lacquer-like technique known as *barniz de pasto*. The chest is decorated with tropical vegetation and animals, including armadillos, jaguars, and small crocodiles known as caimans. The locking clasp, hinges, and caiman-head handles are crafted of silver and are original to the piece.

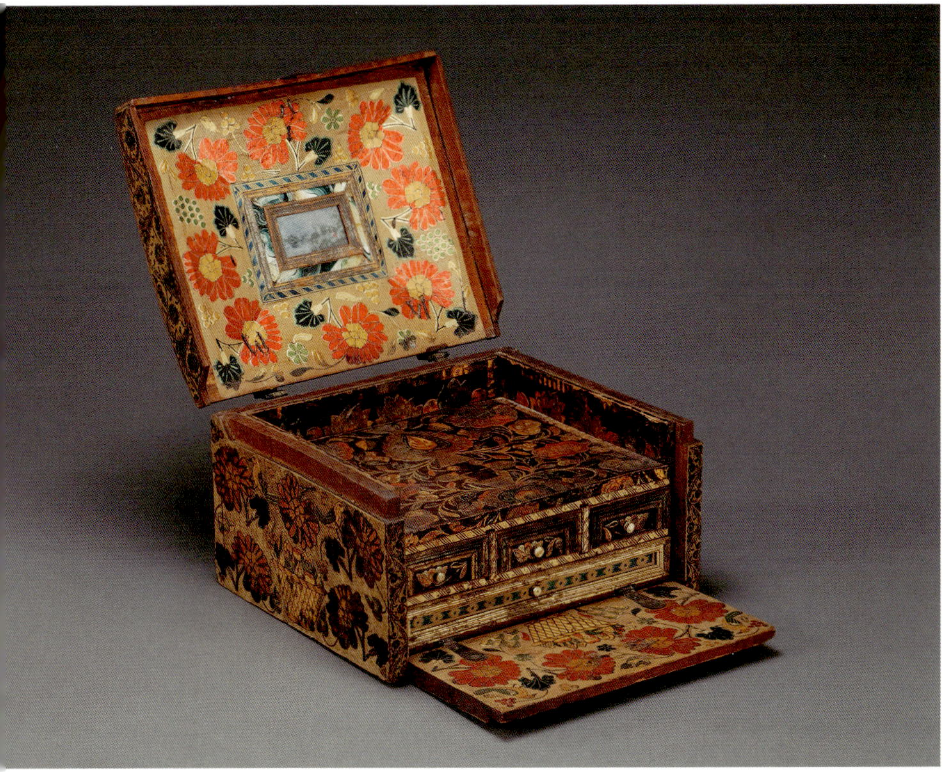

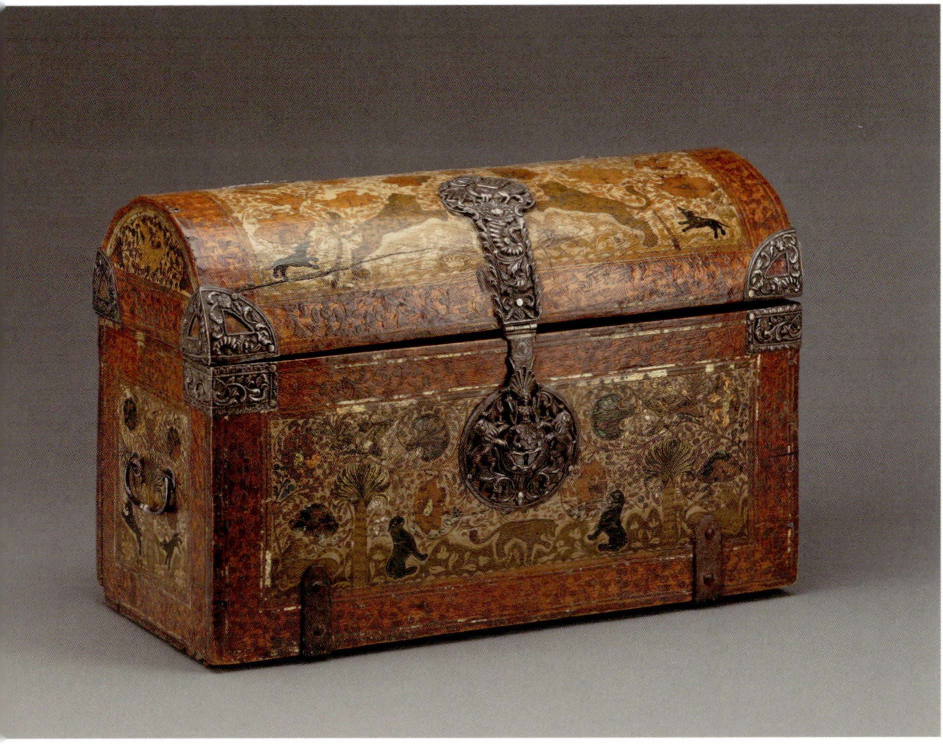

Coral, Pearls, and Beads

*She will be in fashion with her
necklace chain and bracelets of
pearls, and her earrings of some
considerable jewels.*

*—Thomas Gage,
an English Dominican friar,
speaking of women of African
descent in Mexico,
1625–37*

In 1498, Christopher Columbus encountered native women wearing pearl necklaces in Venezuela. By 1528, Nueva Cádiz, the first Spanish town in the Americas, was established on the Venezuelan island of Cubagua to serve as a center for pearl harvesting. Pearls were exported to Spain in such tremendous quantities that when native Peruvian author Garcilaso de la Vega visited Seville in the late 1500s, he commented that "pearls from Venezuela are sold in a heap, as if they were some kind of seed."

Coral was also abundant in the New World. Coral and pearls were harvested during the colonial period at numerous locations in the Atlantic between Florida and Venezuela and in the Pacific between California and Ecuador. Both were so readily available that women of all classes in Mexico and South America wore multistrand pearl and coral bracelets, necklaces, and earrings throughout the colonial era.

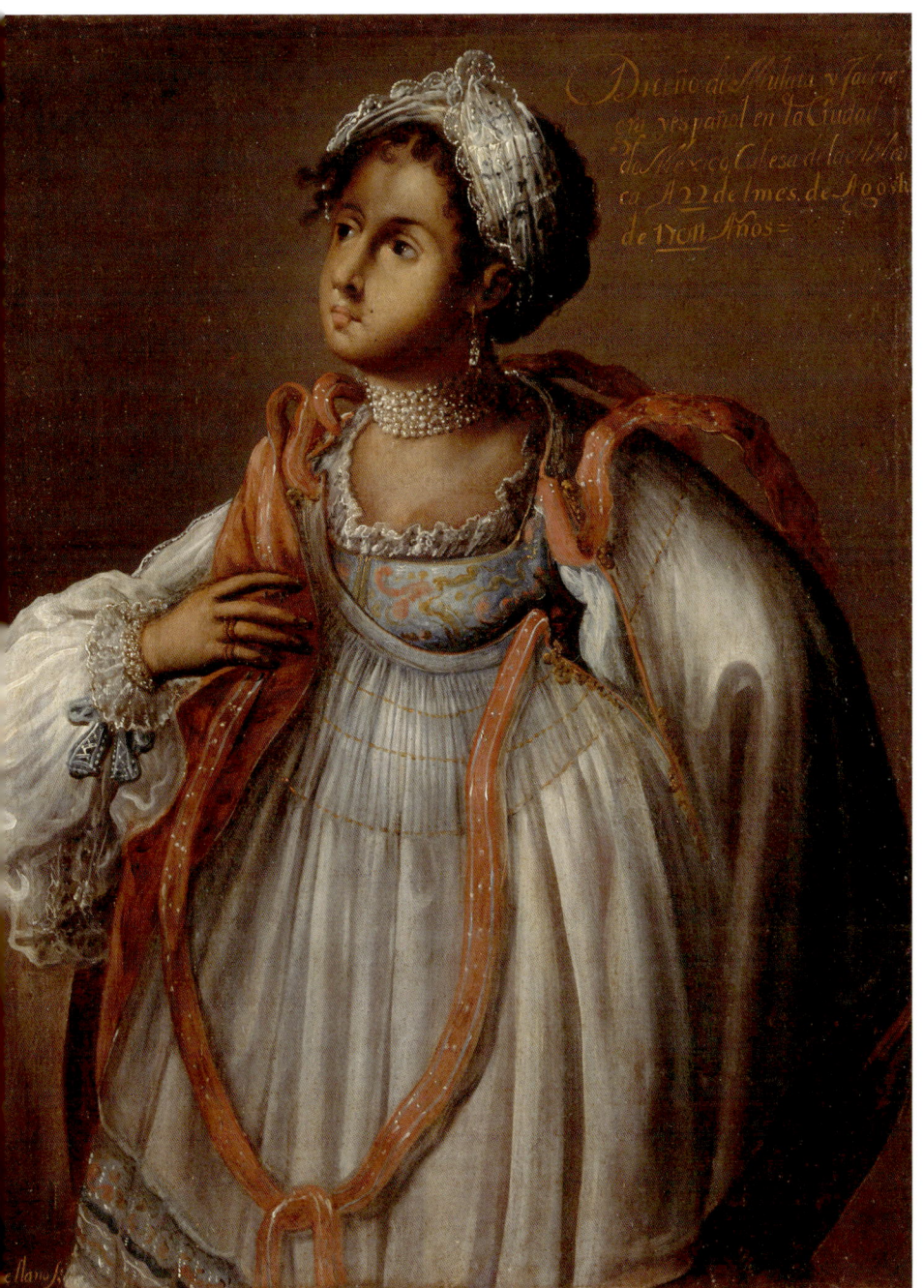

Manuel de Arellano
(active 1691–about 1722)

Rendering of a Mulatta

Mexico, 1711
Oil paint on canvas
39½ x 29⅛ in.
Collection of Frederick and Jan Mayer;
16.2014

According to the inscription, this
woman is the daughter of a black
woman and a Spanish man in
Mexico City. She wears a lace-edged
head scarf, Mexican shawl (*rebozo*),
and a distinctive overblouse (*manga*)
worn exclusively by women of
African descent. Despite her lower
social standing, she wears elaborate
jewelry, including a six-strand pearl
choker, pearl earrings, and multiple
coral rings.

Portrait of Doña Micaela Esquibel

Mexico, about 1750
Oil paint on canvas
31¾ x 16½ in.
Gift of Robert J. Stroessner; 1991.1166

This upper-class woman wears a
pearl choker with large pendant
pearl, a long pearl and coral necklace (possibly a rosary), and gold
and pearl earrings. This portrait
was painted before the death of her
husband, after which she became
a nun and founded the convents
of Santa Coleta and Our Lady of
Guadalupe in Mexico City.

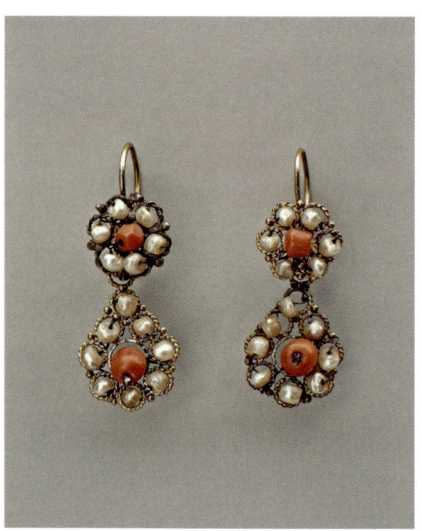

Pair of Earrings

Ecuador or Colombia, 1800s
Gold, coral, and pearls
Gift of the Stapleton Foundation of
Latin American Colonial Art, made
possible by the Renchard family;
1990.622a, b

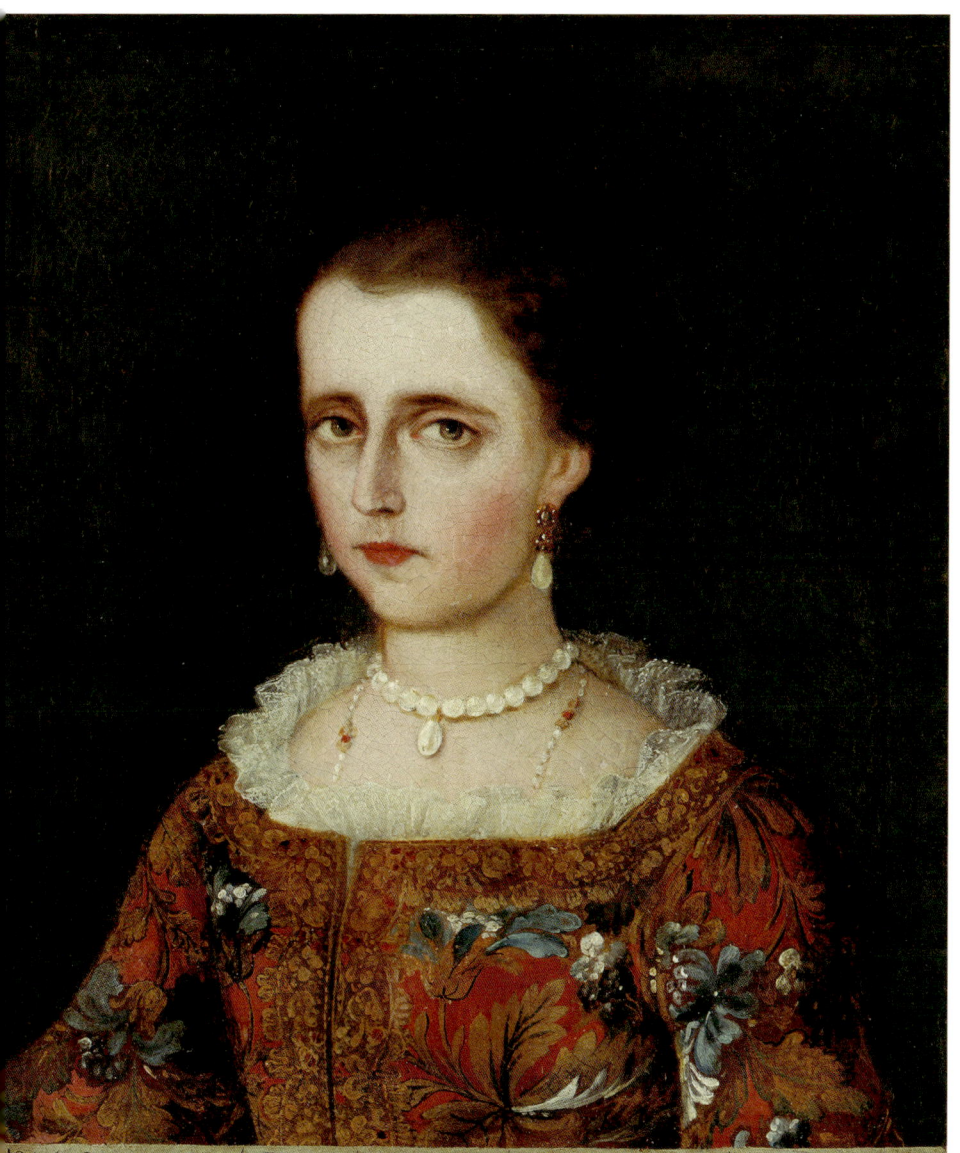

.^{to} de la Sᵗᵃ. Dᵃ Micaela Esquibel. Mᵉ que fue de Nᵗᵗ̃a. M.R.M. Aᵇᵇᵃ. Sor Maria Ana
Fundadora del Convento de Sᵗᵃ Coleta, y pobres Capuchinas de Nᵗᵗ̃a. Sᵗ̃a. de Guada
lupe.

De Indio y Mestiza sale Coyote (Indian and Mestiza Make Coyote)

Mexico, mid 1700s
Oil paint on canvas
31½ x 41 in.
Gift of the Collection of Frederick and Jan Mayer; 2014.218

At the beginning of the 1700s, a new and unique genre of painting, known as *castas*, developed in Mexico. Designed to depict and classify racial mixtures between Spaniards, Africans, and Indians, these paintings contain a wealth of information on the daily life of the era.

In this *casta* painting of a predominantly native family selling birds for the table, the woman wears a gauze-work *huipil* (native overblouse) with coral necklace and earrings.

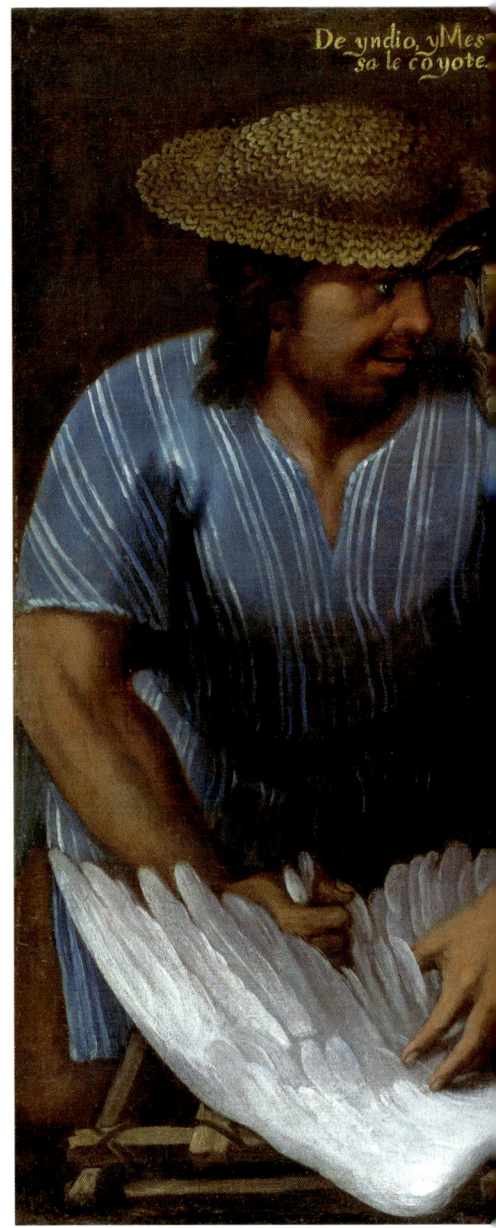

De yndio, y Mes sa le coyote.

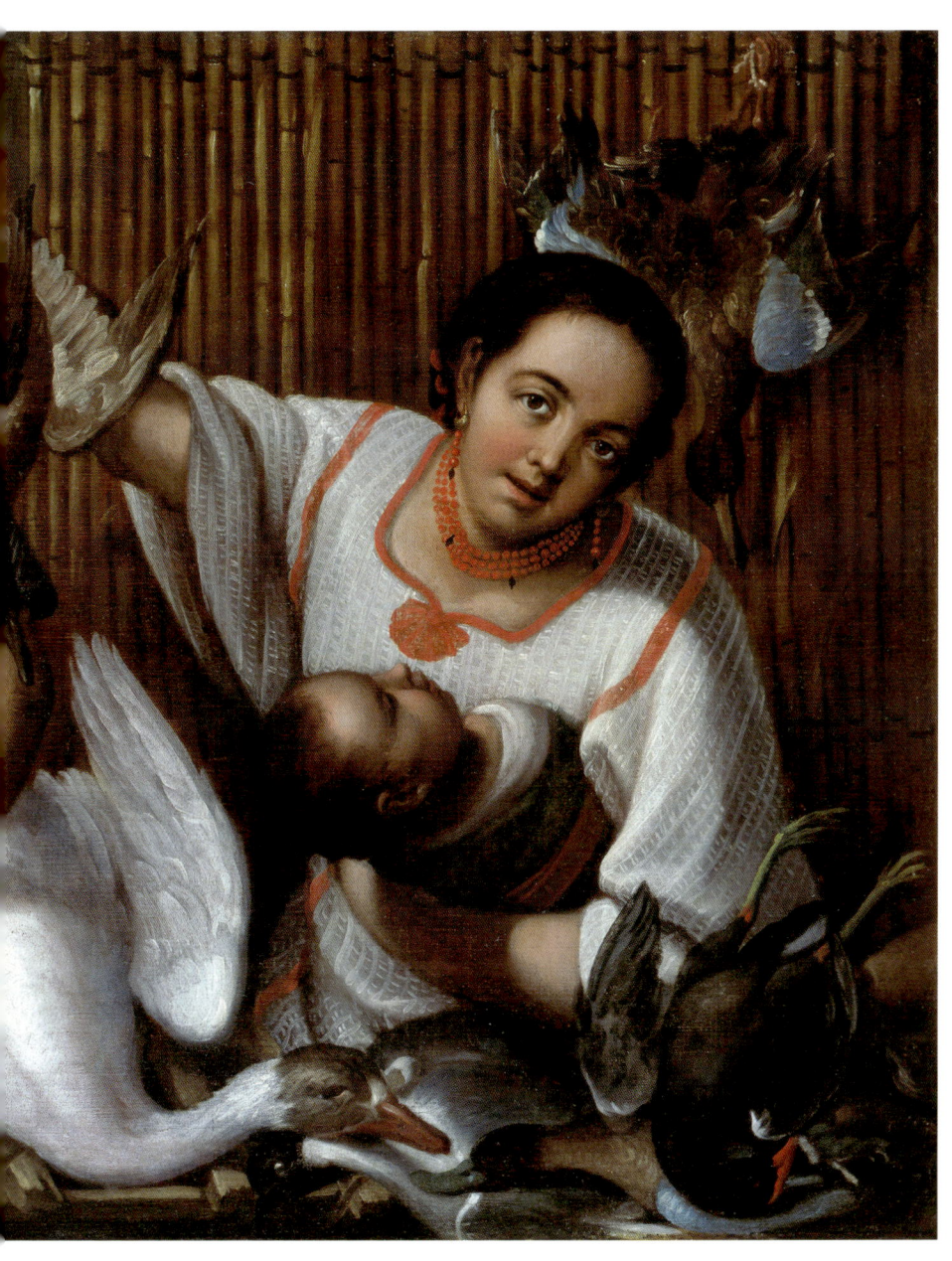

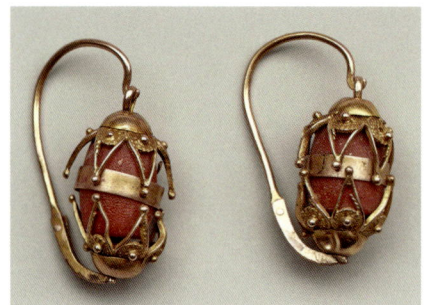

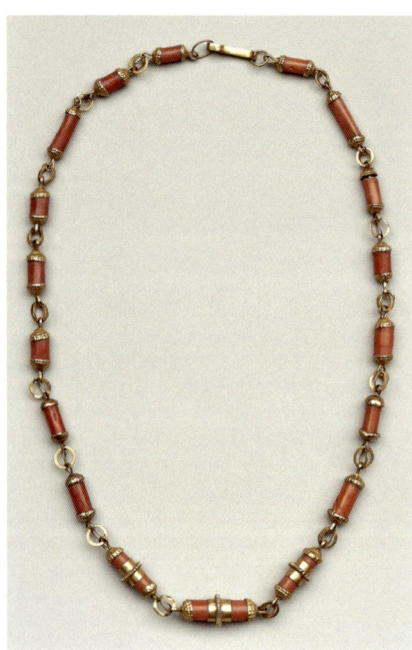

(left)

Earrings and Necklace

Mexico, about 1800
Gold and coral
1¼ x ¾ in. (each)
18⅞ in. long
Gift of Robert J. Stroessner;
1989.211.1, .2

(opposite)

Portrait of María Josefa Brito

Yucatán, Mexico, about 1790
Oil paint on canvas
5⅞ x 4½ in.
Gift of the Collection of Frederick
and Jan Mayer; 2013.378

This young woman holds a fan and wears pearl and green-glass bead bracelets, a black ribbon choker embellished with coral and silver or diamonds, and coral earrings. Her hairstyle, decorated with blue, white, and red feathers, is reminiscent of the elaborate up-dos worn by the French queen Marie Antoinette (1755–1793).

Late in the colonial period, small, personal traveling portraits became common, such as this one. The painting is inscribed in the upper left, "In the province of Yucatán, Doña María Josefa Brito." The small card she holds in her hand reads, "To my dearest husband, Don Manuel Brito."

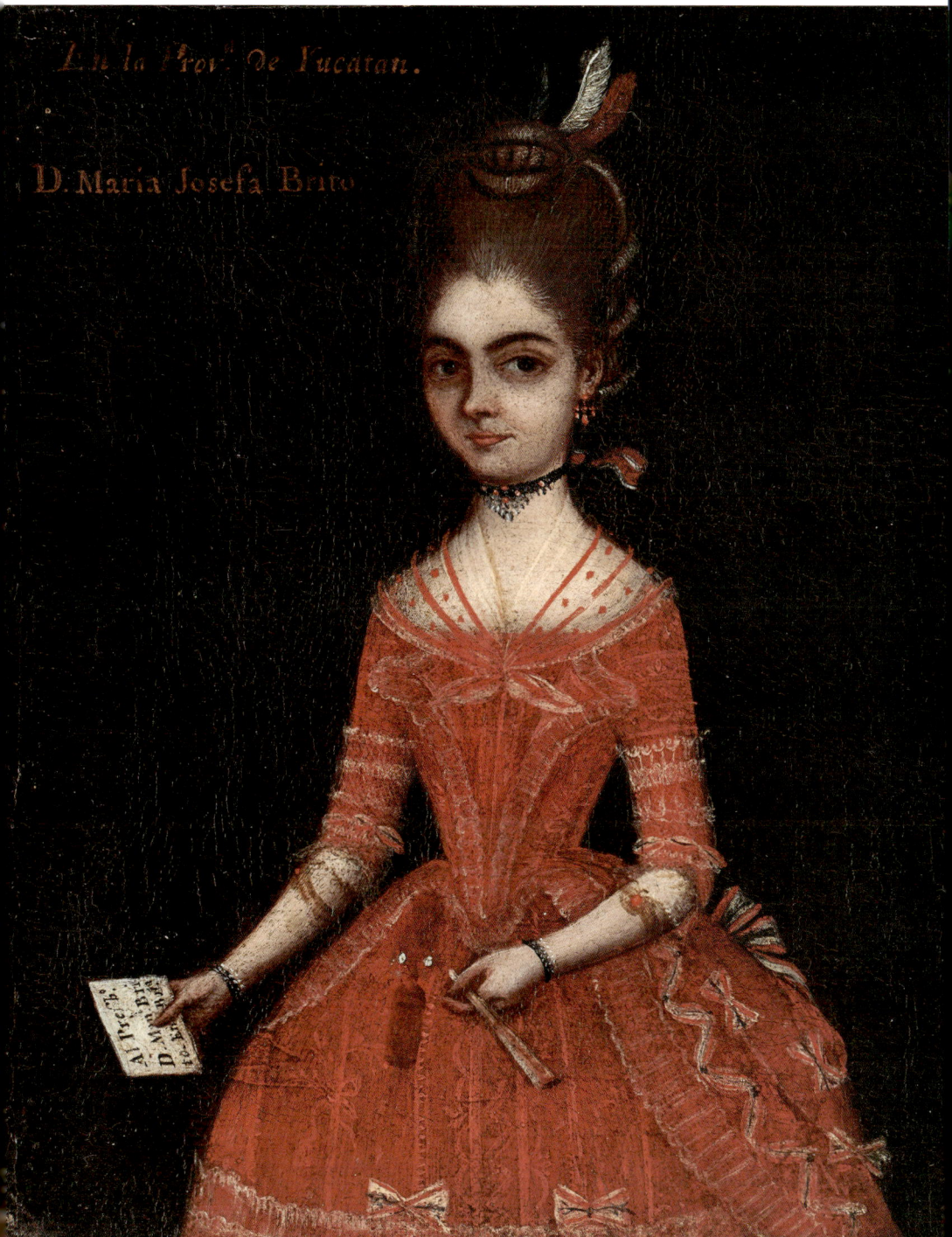

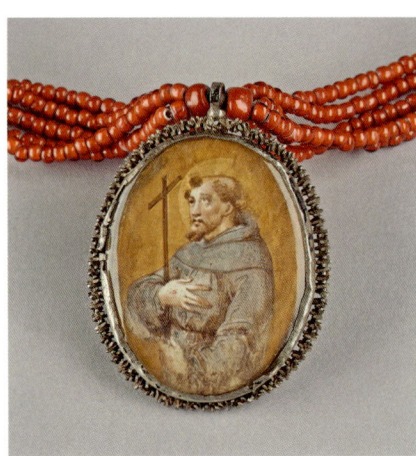

(opposite, and detail of reverse shown at left)

Necklace with Double-sided Pendant

Mexico, 1700s
Glass beads, silver, and paint on parchment
20½ x 2½ in.
Gift of Mr. and Mrs. James M. Jeter;
1985.358

The role of beads as a desirable item traded by Europeans with Native Americans is well known; Columbus brought green and yellow glass beads to be traded on his voyages. Although glass beads were produced by the major glass industries in Venice, France, and the Netherlands, most beads brought to the New World by Spaniards were probably made in Venice or Spain. A glass factory was operating in Puebla, Mexico, by 1542.

Spaniards and Indians alike used glass beads to make rosaries and jewelry. Here a silver frame encloses a double-sided pendant with miniature paintings of the Virgin Mary with the Christ Child on one side and Saint Francis on the other (see detail at left). It hangs from a multistrand necklace of red glass beads with white centers. Known as white-hearts, this type of bead was a staple in colonial-era trade.

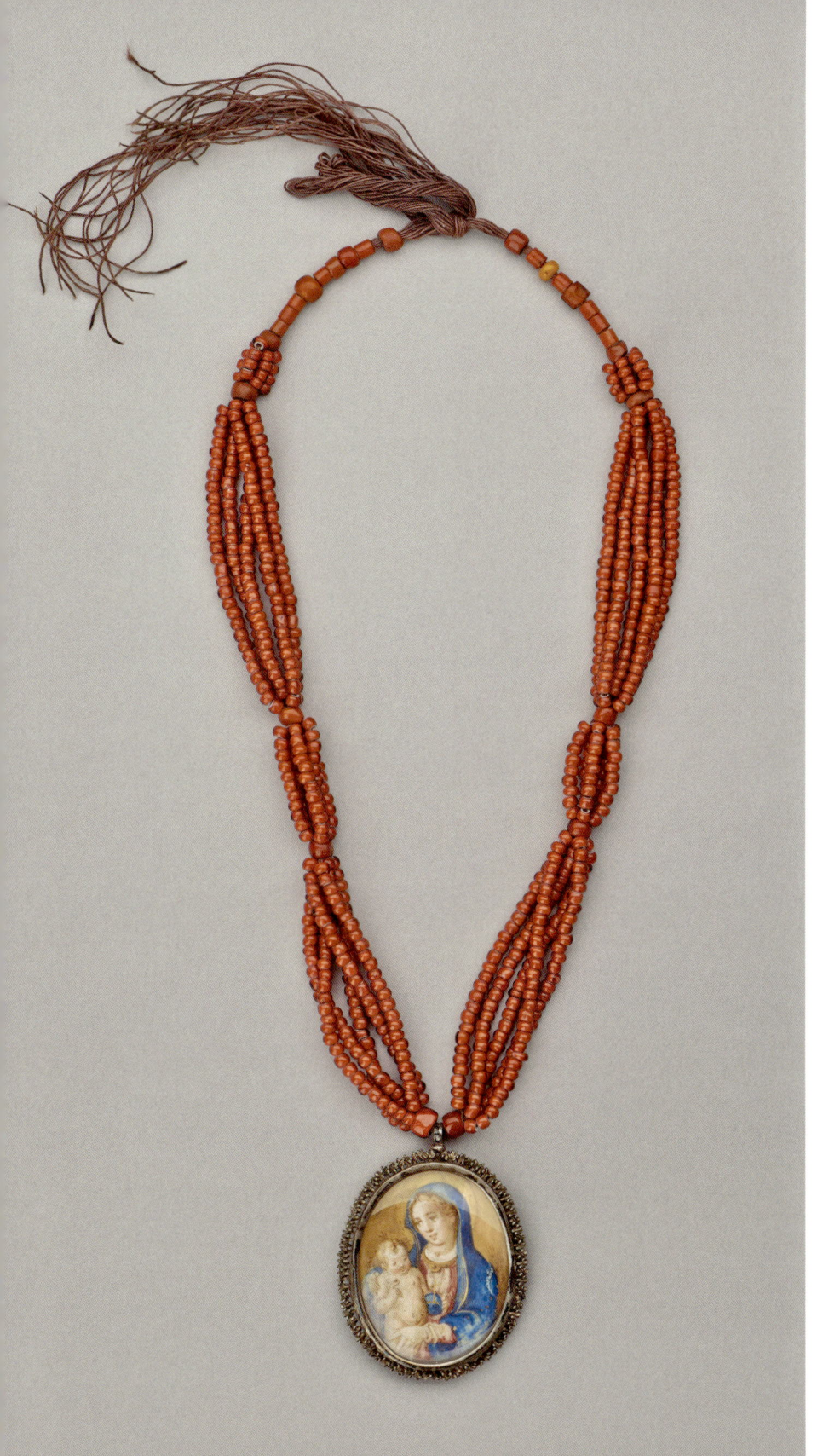

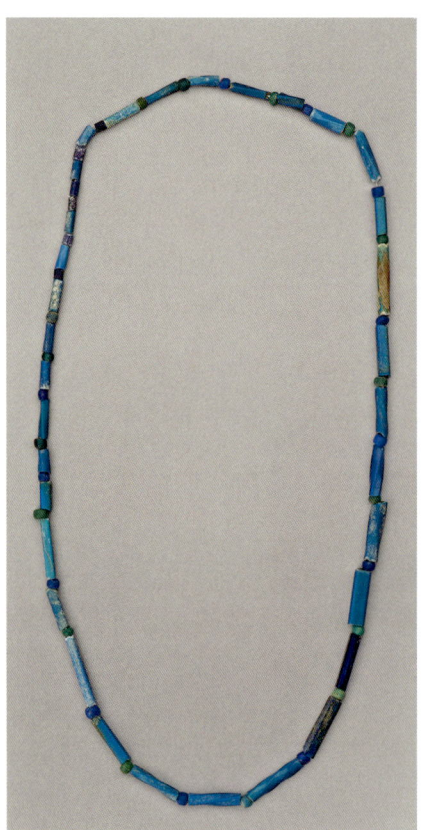

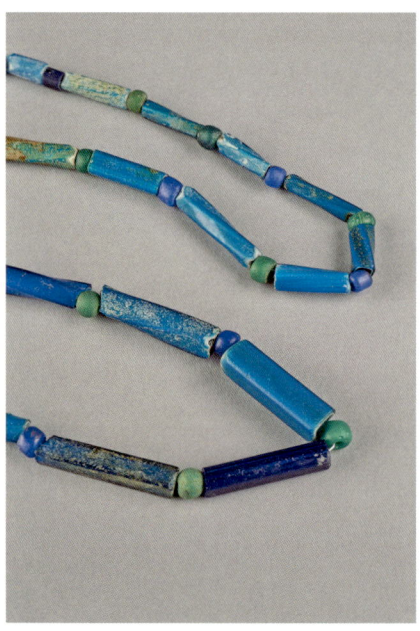

(top, and detail, bottom)

Nueva Cádiz Beads

Spain, 1500s
Glass
34 in. long
Gift of the Collection of Frederick
and Jan Mayer; 2013.329

Some of the earliest glass beads used in the Spanish Americas, and certainly the most prized, were Nueva Cádiz beads, so named by modern archaeologists for the site in Venezuela where many were found. Here the long Nueva Cádiz Twisted and Nueva Cádiz Plain turquoise-over-white beads are separated by small green-glass seed beads, one of the most common types of beads.

(opposite)

Woman and boy of Patagonia in South America receiving beads from Admiral Byron

London, about 1782
Engraving on paper
11½ x 7 in.
Gift of the Collection of Frederick
and Jan Mayer; 2013.382

All Europeans used glass beads as gifts or trade items in the Americas. Here the British admiral Lord John Byron gives beads to Patagonians in the region near the tip of South America. He was shipwrecked there in 1741 and passed through there again on his round-the-world voyage in 1766.

London Published by Alexr Hogg at the Kings Arms No 16 Paternoster Row.

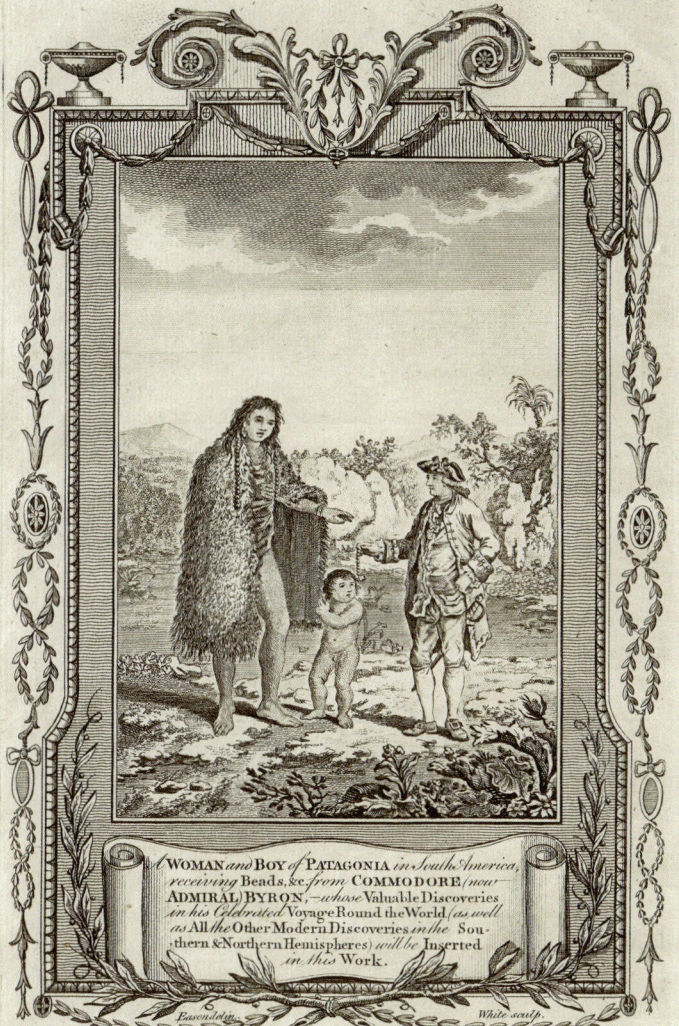

A WOMAN and BOY of PATAGONIA in South America,
receiving Beads, &c from COMMODORE (now
ADMIRAL) BYRON, — whose Valuable Discoveries
in his Celebrated Voyage Round the World (as well
as All the Other Modern Discoveries in the Sou-
thern & Northern Hemispheres) will be Inserted
in this Work.

Easendel?   White sculp.

Sacred Adornment

The riches belonging to the altars are infinite in price and value ... candlesticks, jewels belonging to the saints, and crowns of gold and silver.
—Thomas Gage,
an English Dominican friar,
speaking of churches in Mexico City,
1625

When the Spanish colonized the Americas, they brought Catholic missionaries to spread the faith. They built cathedrals, churches, monasteries, and convents and commissioned portraits of the clergy. Just like secular portraits, these paintings of clerics and nuns showed signs of prosperity in the Americas. Priests wore opulent vestments with gold crucifixes and rosaries. Nuns attached miniature paintings of the Virgin Mary and saints, crafted into brooches called nun's badges, onto their habits.

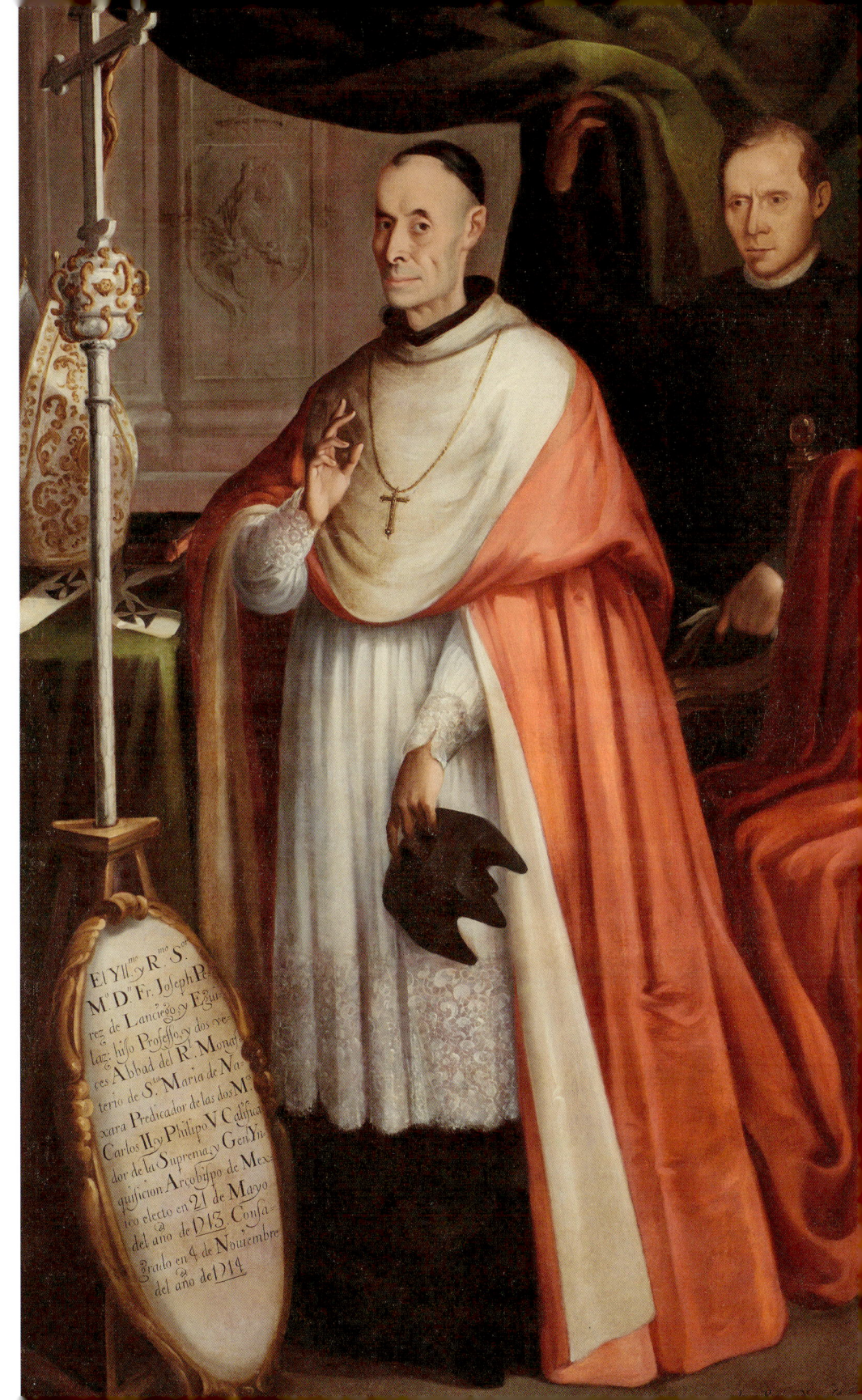

El Yll.me y R.mo S.or
M.o D.r Fr. Joseph Pe
rez de Lanciego y Egui
laz: hijo Professo, y dos ve
ces Abbad del R.l Monas
terio de S.ta Maria de Na
xara Predicador de las dos M
Carlos II, y Rey Philipo V. C difica
dor de la Suprema, y Gen.l Yn
quisicion Arçobispo de Mex
ico electo en 21 de Mayo
del año de 1713. Consa
grado en 4 de Nouiembre
del año de 1714

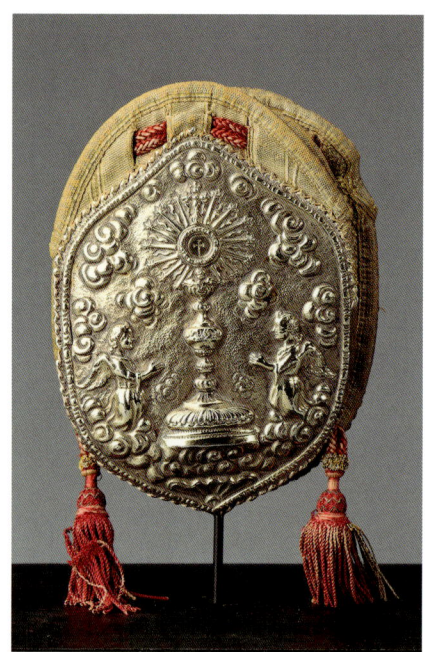

(previous page)

Juan Rodríguez Juárez
(1667–1734)

Portrait of
Archbishop Don Francisco José
Pérez de Lanciego y Eguilaz

Mexico, 1714
Oil paint on canvas
81½ x 48¾ in.
Gift of the Collection of Frederick
and Jan Mayer; 2013.350

Male clergy wore jewelry and
owned jeweled accessories associated with their rank. Here the
Archbishop of Mexico wears a
gold necklace with a cross, possibly
set with stones. In front of him is a
gold and silver processional crucifix. The archbishop is shown here
with his nephew, who accompanied
him to the New World.

(opposite, and reverse shown at left)

Bishop's Bag or Alms Bag

Mexico, about 1780
Silver, silk and gold thread fabric, silk
lining and tassels
8⅜ x 5¾ in.
Gift of the Collection of Frederick
and Jan Mayer; 2013.311

On one side of the red silk and gold
thread bag is a silver plaque bearing
the monogram of the Virgin Mary
(right); on the other side two kneel-
ing angels flank a large monstrance
(above left), the vessel used to display the sacred wafer of Christ.

Sacred Adornment

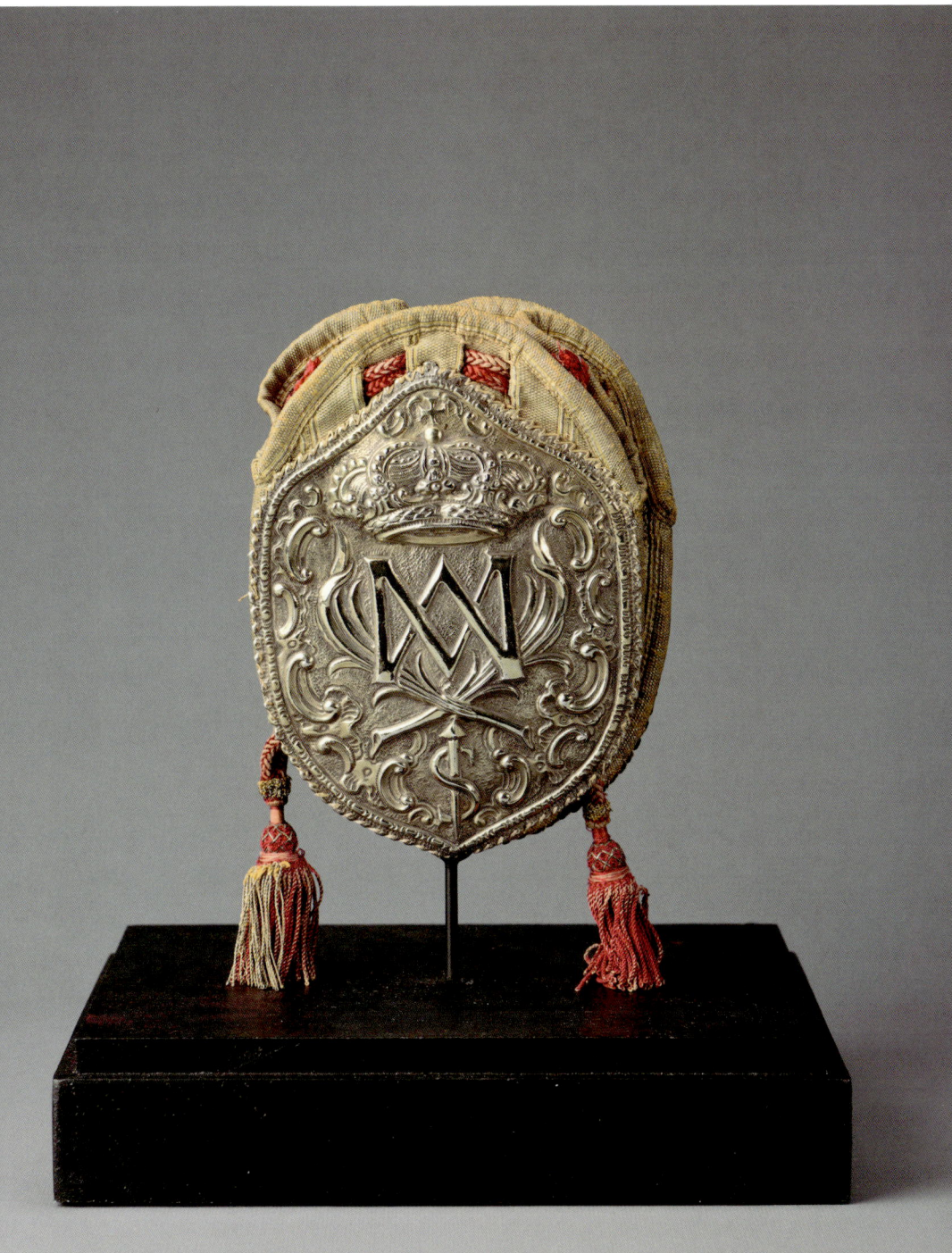

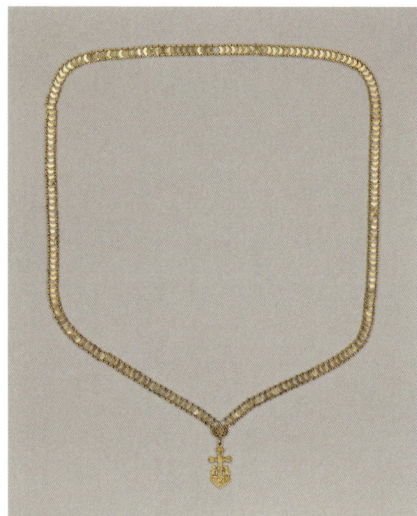

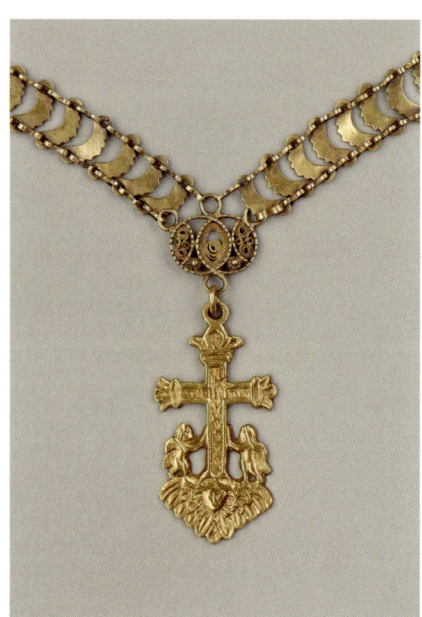

Necklace with Cross

Ecuador or Colombia, 1800s
Gold
21¼ x 1 in.
Gift of the Stapleton Foundation of
Latin American Colonial Art, made
possible by the Renchard family;
1990.617

This long gold chain, known in
Spanish as a *soquilla*, is expertly
crafted and elaborately linked. Two
angels flank the gold cross pendant.

(opposite)

Attributed to
Diego de Cuentas

Portrait of Archbishop Fray Felipe Galindo Chávez y Pineda

Guadalajara, Mexico, about 1700
Oil paint on canvas
80½ x 50½ in.
Collection of Frederick and Jan Mayer;
4.2011

The Archbishop of Guadalajara
wears a cross set with jewels, possibly emeralds, suspended from a
gold chain. A long beaded rosary
hangs from his waist, and on his
right hand is a gold ring set with a
stone. A bishop's miter (hat) decorated with six jeweled pins is seen
to his right. His accomplishments
are outlined in the scroll in the lower left, and his tasseled family coat
of arms appears at upper left.

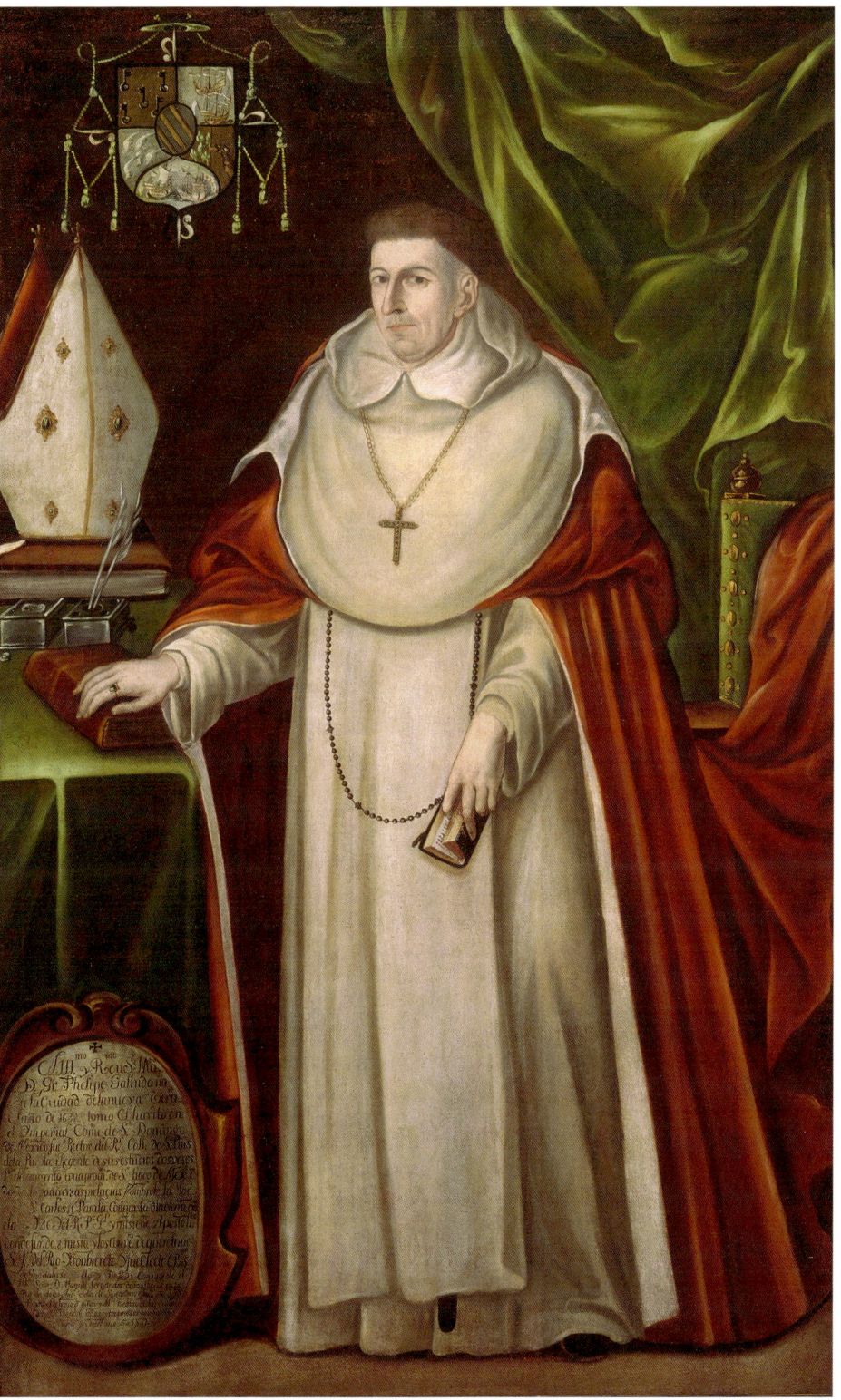

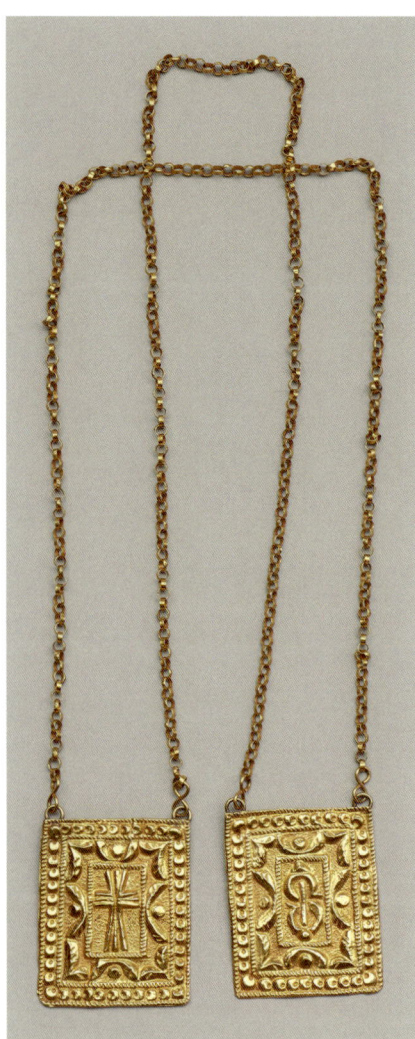

(left)

Scapular

Ecuador or Colombia, 1800s
Gold
Gift of the Stapleton Foundation of
Latin American Colonial Art, made
possible by the Renchard family;
1990.621

A scapular is worn like a necklace,
with one rectangle hanging in front
and the other in back. This ham-
mered gold scapular has a cross on
one end, and on the other, a nail en-
closed by an "S" for *esclavo*, or slave,
symbolizing the wearer's devotion.

(opposite)

Signed by Miguel Jerónimo Zendejas (1723–1815)

Our Lady of Mt. Carmel

Puebla, Mexico, 1772
Oil paint on canvas
42 x 30 in.
Gift of the Collection of Frederick
and Jan Mayer; 2013.304

According to legend, the Virgin
Mary appeared to Christian hermits
who lived on Mt. Carmel in the
Holy Land and gave them a cloak
called a scapular. Later, miniature
scapulars that look like double-
ended necklaces (above left) were
worn by the faithful as a reminder
of personal religious devotion. Both
the Virgin and the Christ Child in
this painting hold scapulars.

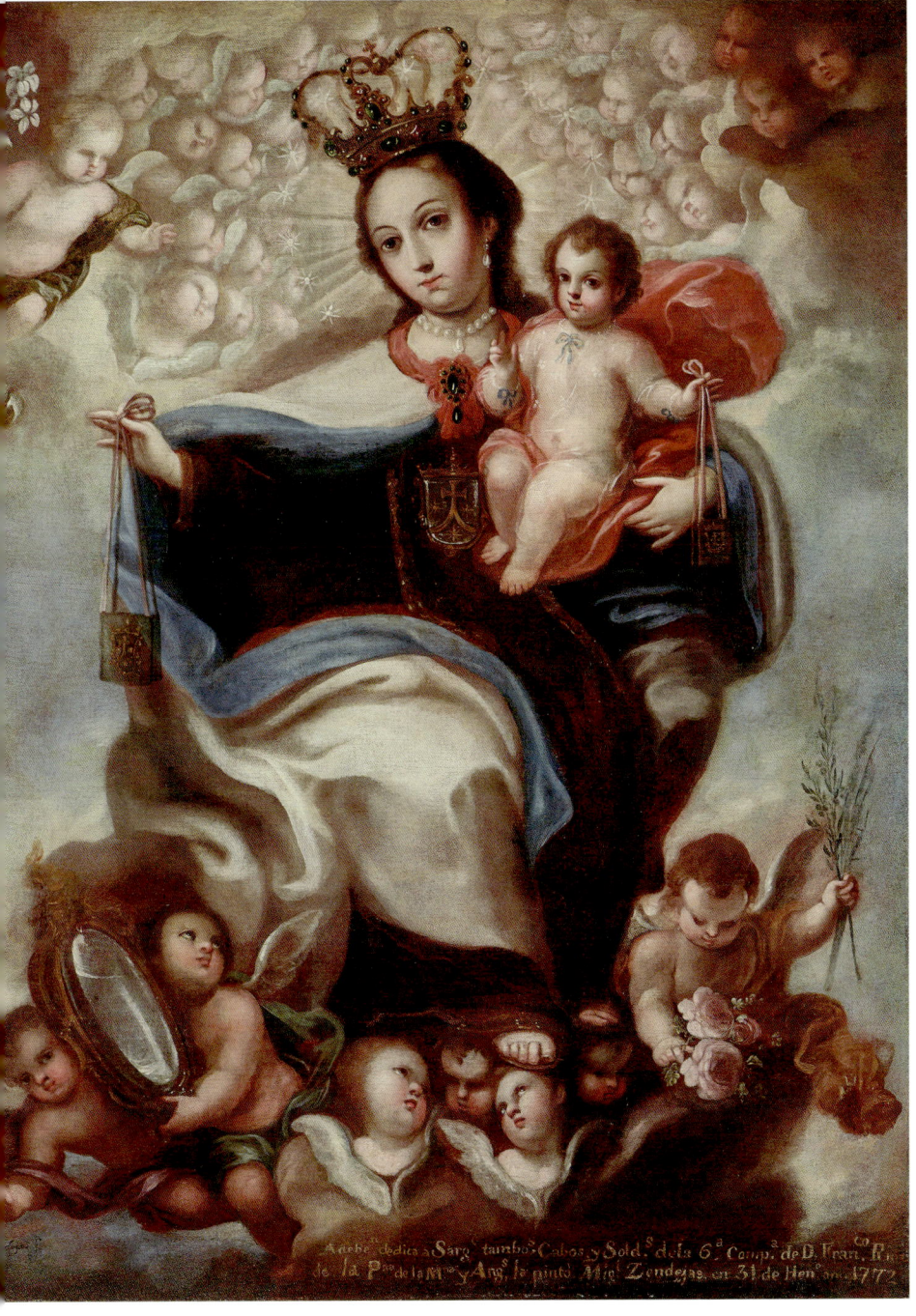

A este se dedica a Sarg.tos tambos Cabos, y Sold.s de la 6.ª Comp.ª de D. Fran.co R.l
de la P.za de la M.ª y A.os la pintó Mig.l Zendejas en 31 de Hen.º año 1772

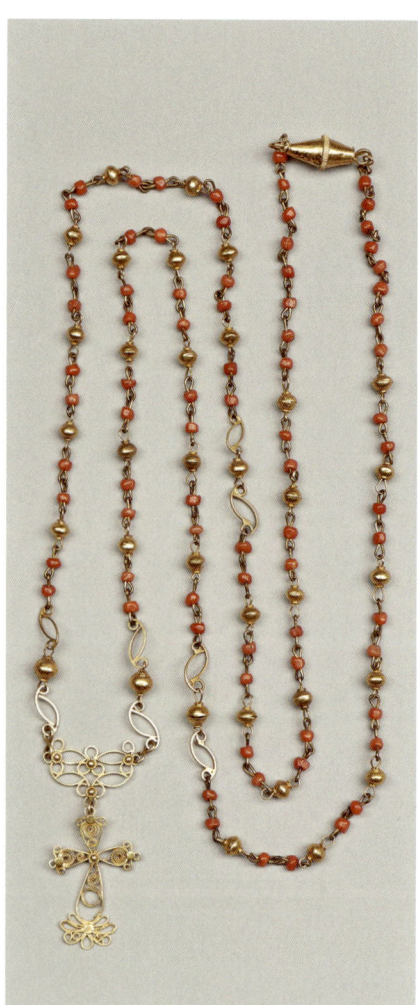

(left)

Rosary

Ecuador or Colombia, 1800s
Gold and coral
18 x ½ in.
Gift of the Stapleton Foundation of
Latin American Colonial Art, made
possible by the Renchard family;
1990.613

The rosary, a form of prayer beads,
guides the faithful through sets of
prayers. This rosary is crafted of
gold filigree and tiny coral beads.
While prayer beads are common
in many religions, Christian use of
them starts to be common around
1000. The rosary is most often
associated with Saint Dominic (right).

(opposite)

Signed by Antonio de Arellano (active 1670–1710)

Virgin and Christ Child Giving a Rosary to Saint Dominic

Mexico, about 1700
Oil paint on canvas
49½ x 38½ in.
Gift of the Collection of Frederick
and Jan Mayer; 2013.348

In this painting the Virgin Mary
hands a rosary to St. Dominic, who
is credited with introducing rosaries
to Christian devotion. The Virgin
and Christ Child both hold pearl
rosaries and wear gold crowns set
with jewels.

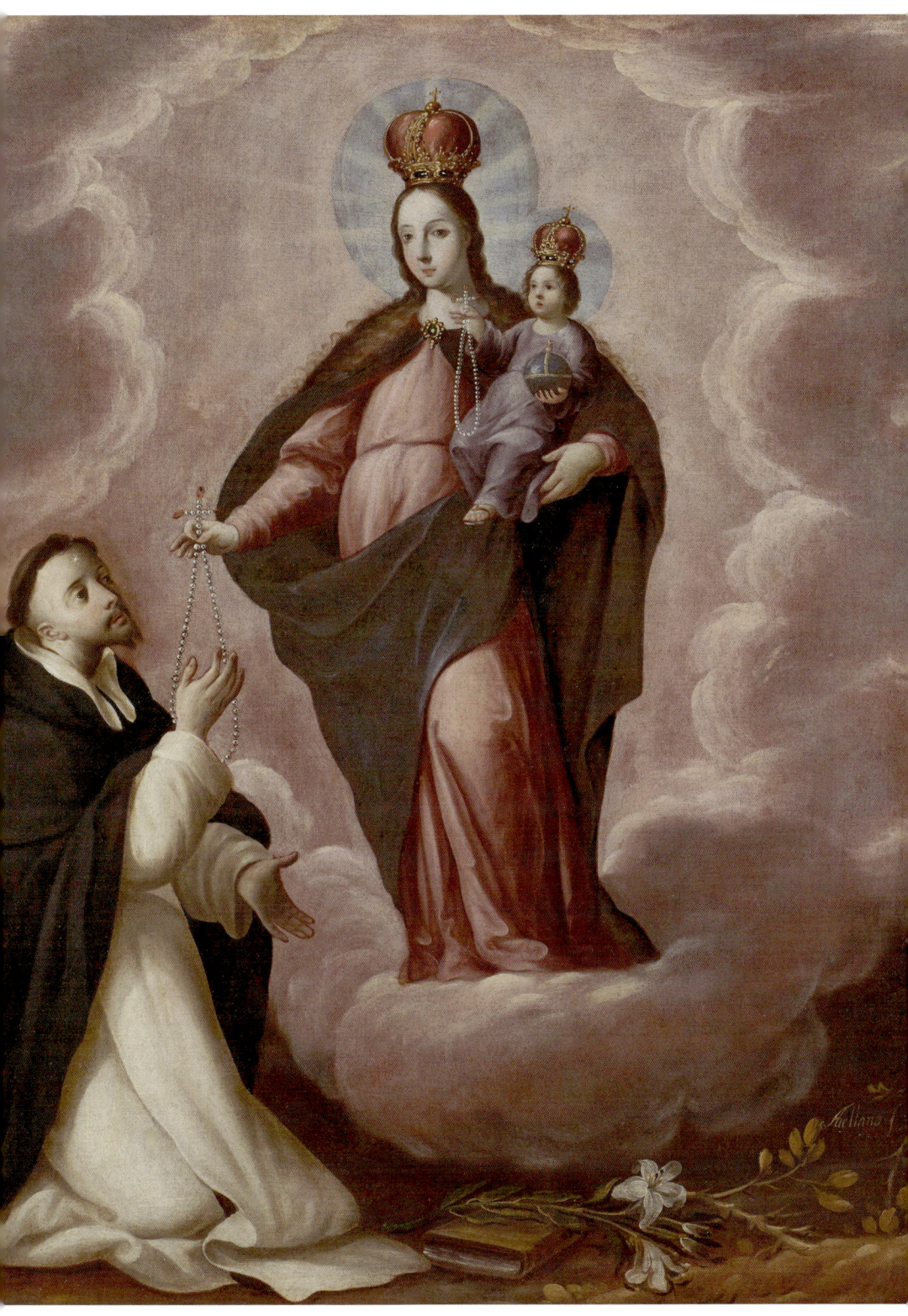

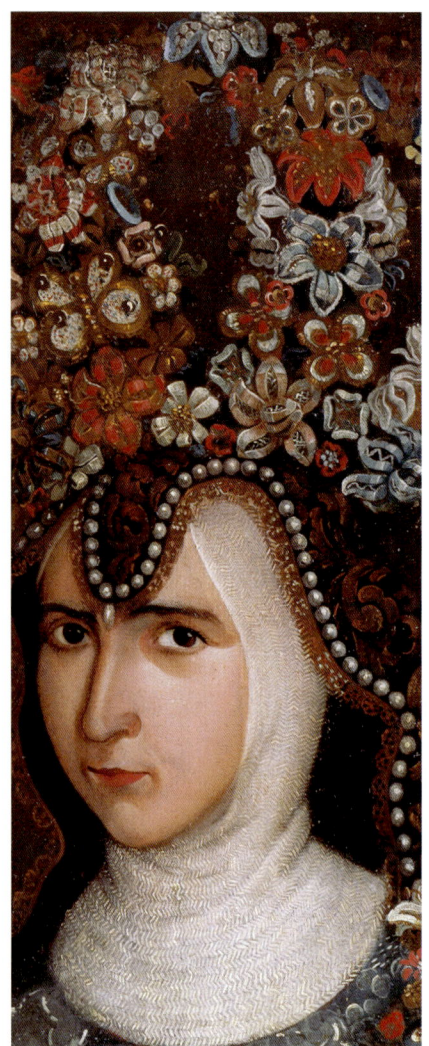

(opposite, and detail left)

Portrait of Sister Ana María of the Precious Blood of Christ

Puebla, Mexico, about 1770
Oil paint on canvas
45 x 35 in.
Gift of the Collection of Frederick
and Jan Mayer; 2014.215

As "brides of Christ," nuns in Mexico took their vows wearing a crown covered with flowers and carrying candles or bouquets with matching flowers. The flowers were made of wax or fabric over a wire framework. In some cases, the nuns saved their crowns and bouquets and were later buried wearing them. According to the inscription, the nun in this portrait was a member of the Franciscan Convent of Santa Clara in Puebla, Mexico.

Her flower headdress is also adorned with pearls. She holds a small sculpture of Christ on the cross, alluding to her new name as a nun: Ana María of the Precious Blood of Christ.

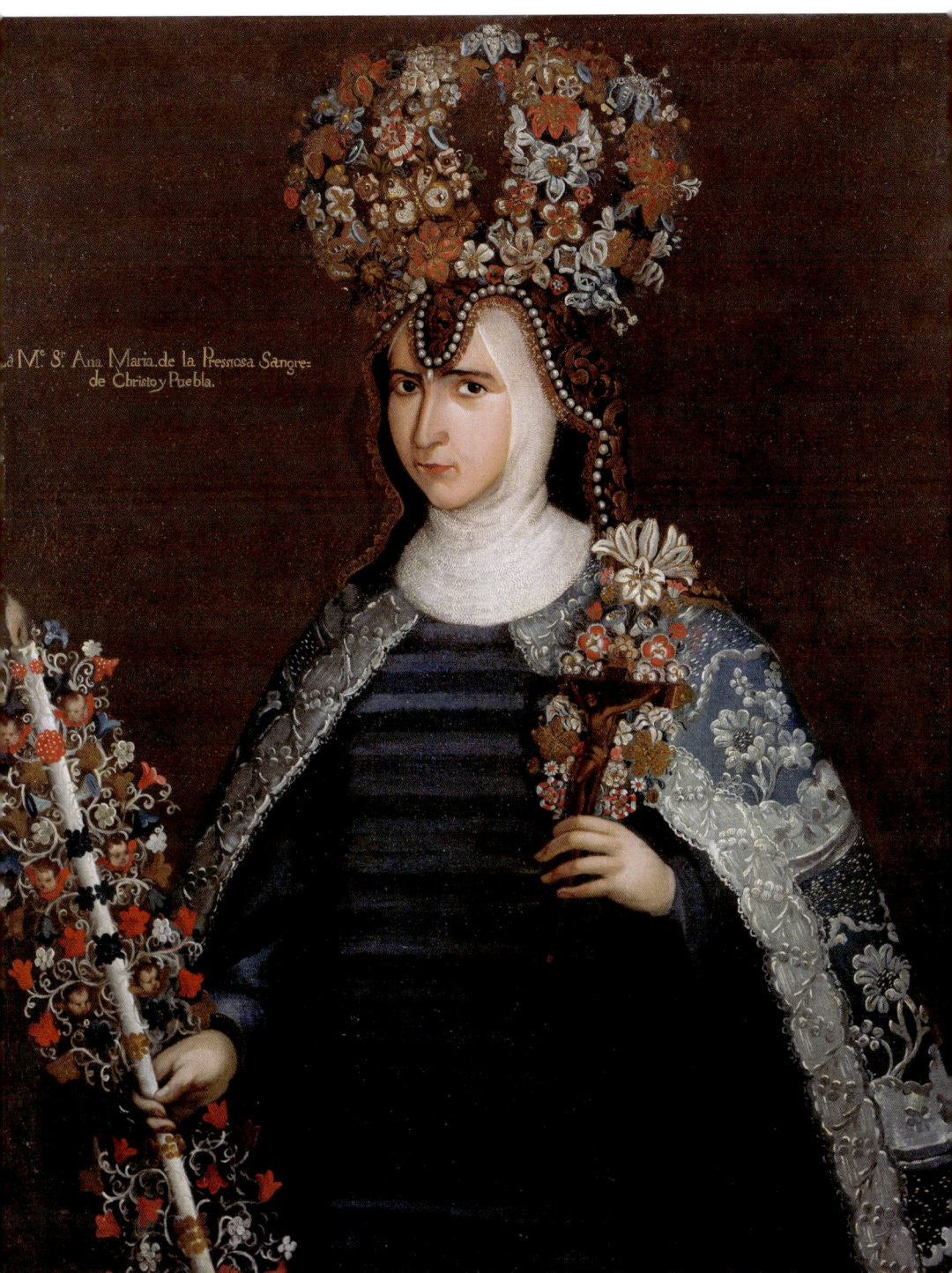

La M.ᵉ Sᵒʳ. Ana Maria de la Pressiosa Sangre= de Christo y Puebla.

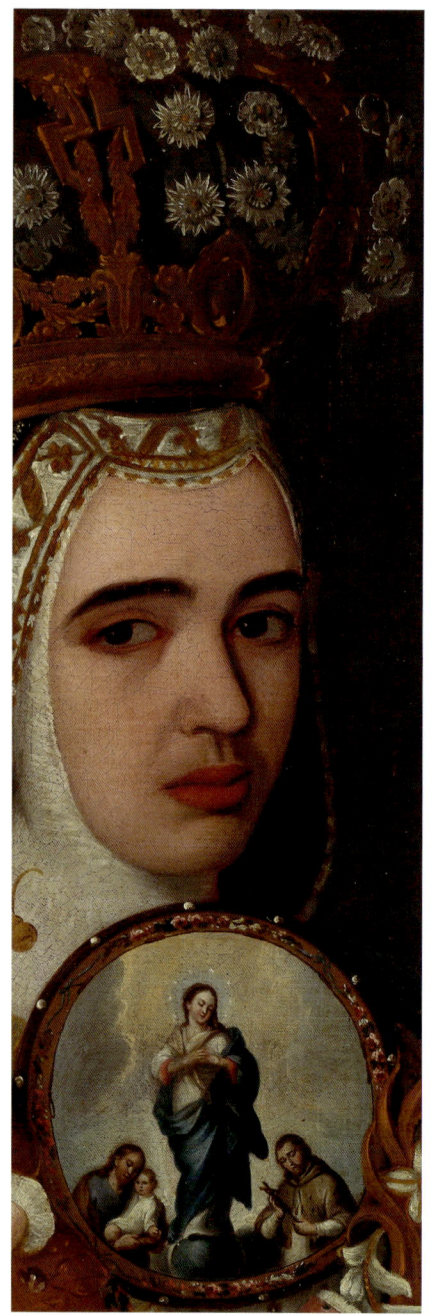

Signed by José de Álcíbar (active 1751–1803)

Portrait of Sor M. María Anna Josefa de San Ignacio

Mexico, 1793
Oil paint on canvas
40¾ x 32⅞ in.
Szépmüvészeti Múzeum, Budapest /
Museum of Fine Arts, 2015

This portrait shows a young woman elaborately dressed to take her vows as a Conceptionist nun in Mexico City. Attached to her collar is a nun's badge (*escudo*), unique to Mexico. Invented there in the late 1600s, they were worn at the throat by Conceptionist and Jeronymite nuns over the habits of their orders.

Bearing images of the Virgin and saints significant to the order and/or the individual nun, these badges were painted on round or oval sheets of copper and framed in tortoiseshell or wood. Many of the most famous artists in Mexico painted these miniature devotional images. Some of the badges shown on the following pages bear their signatures.

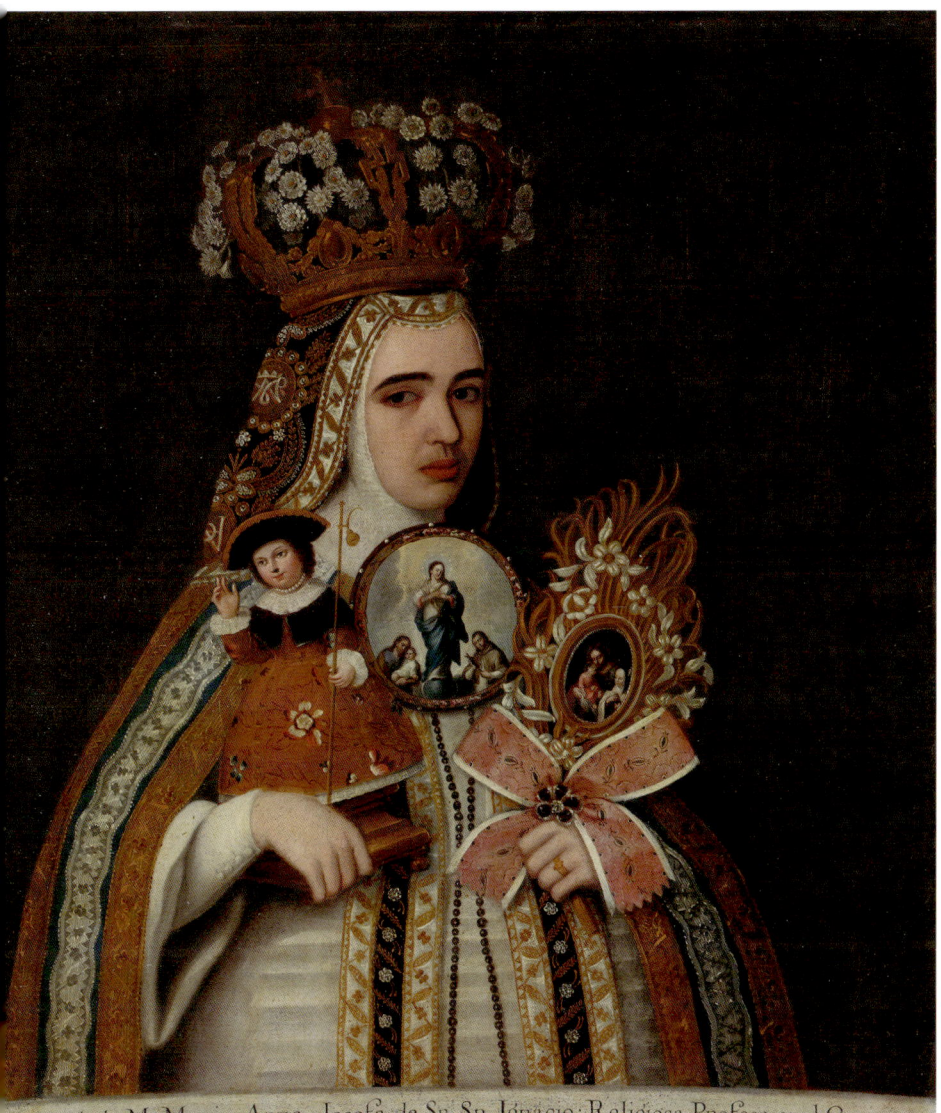

etrato de la M. Maria Anna Josefa de Sr. Sn. Ignacio: Religiosa Profesa en el Convento
Sn. Sn. Jose de Gracia: hija legitima de Dn. José Francisco Ventemilla y de Dña. Maria Garcia. Pro-
Fesó el dia 13. de Octubre de 1795. de 16. años, 13. dias de edad.

Josephus de Alcibar pinx.ᵗ aⁿ 1794.

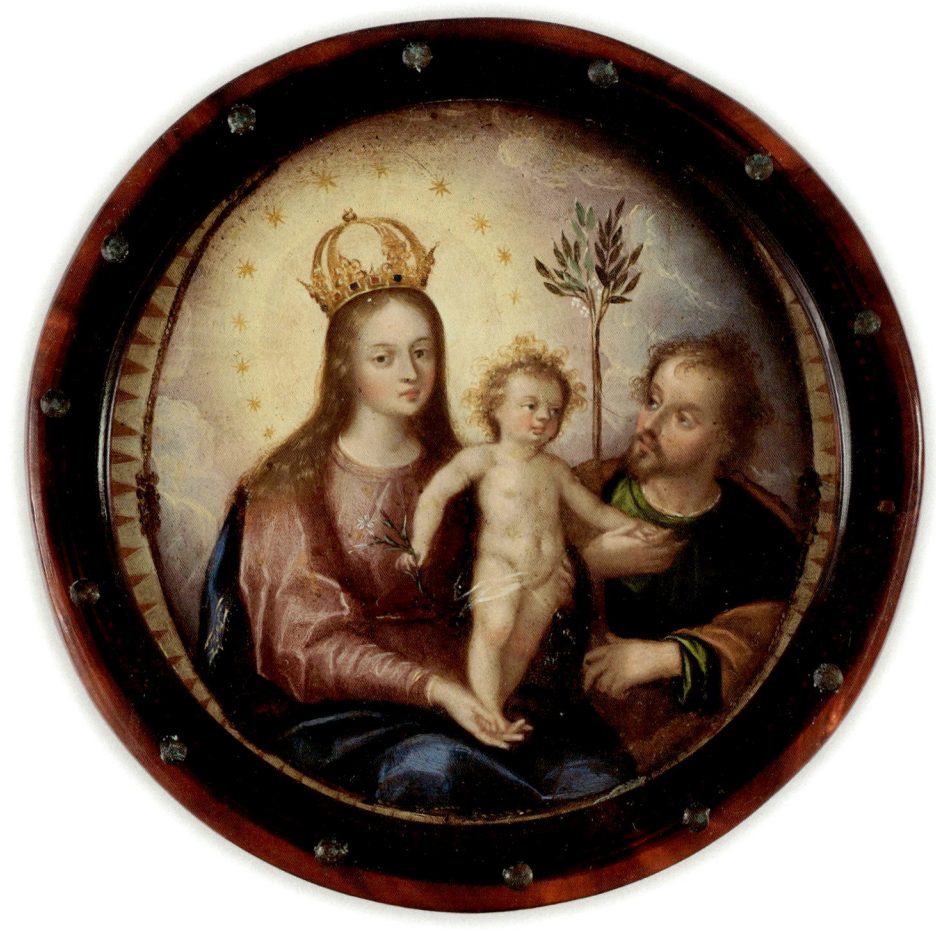

Attributed to Luis Juárez
(active 1610–39)

Holy Family

Mexico, early 1600s
Oil paint and gold leaf on copper;
tortoiseshell frame
4⅔ in. diameter
Gift of the Collection of Frederick
and Jan Mayer; 2013.363

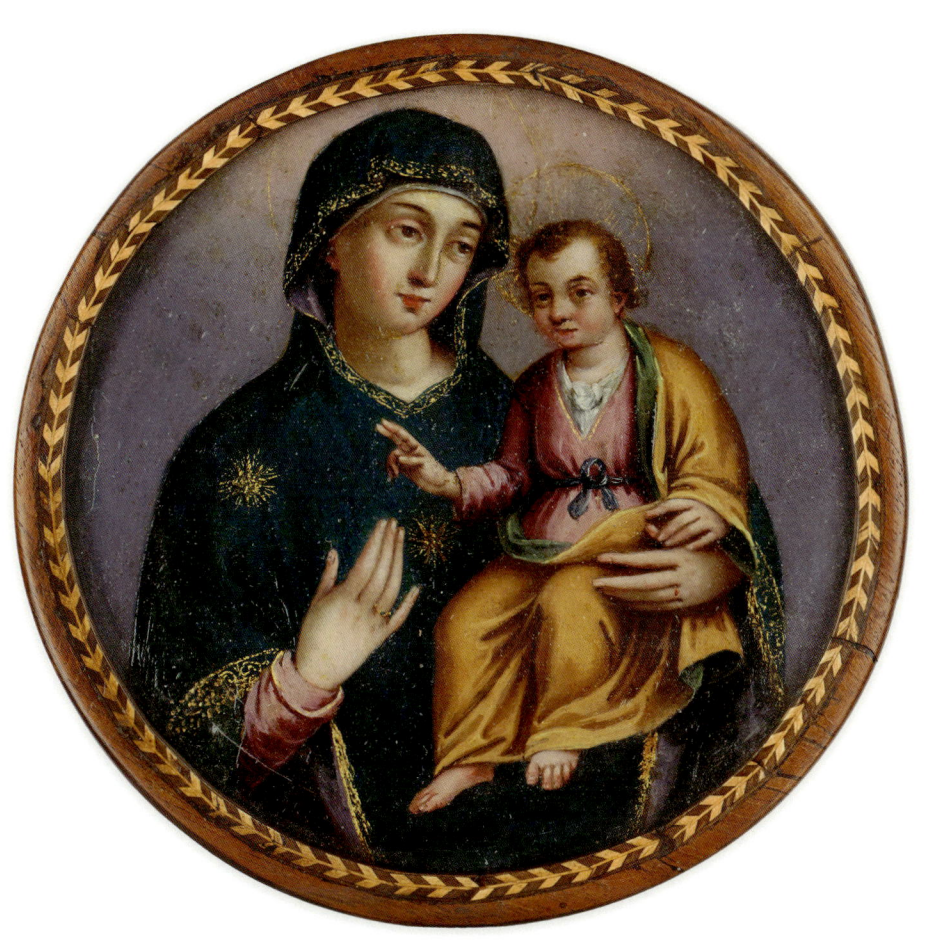

Virgin and Christ Child

Mexico, 1600s
Oil paint and gold leaf on copper;
tortoiseshell and inlaid wood frame
5½ in. diameter
Gift of the United States Fish and
Wildlife Service, Denver, Colorado;
2005.92

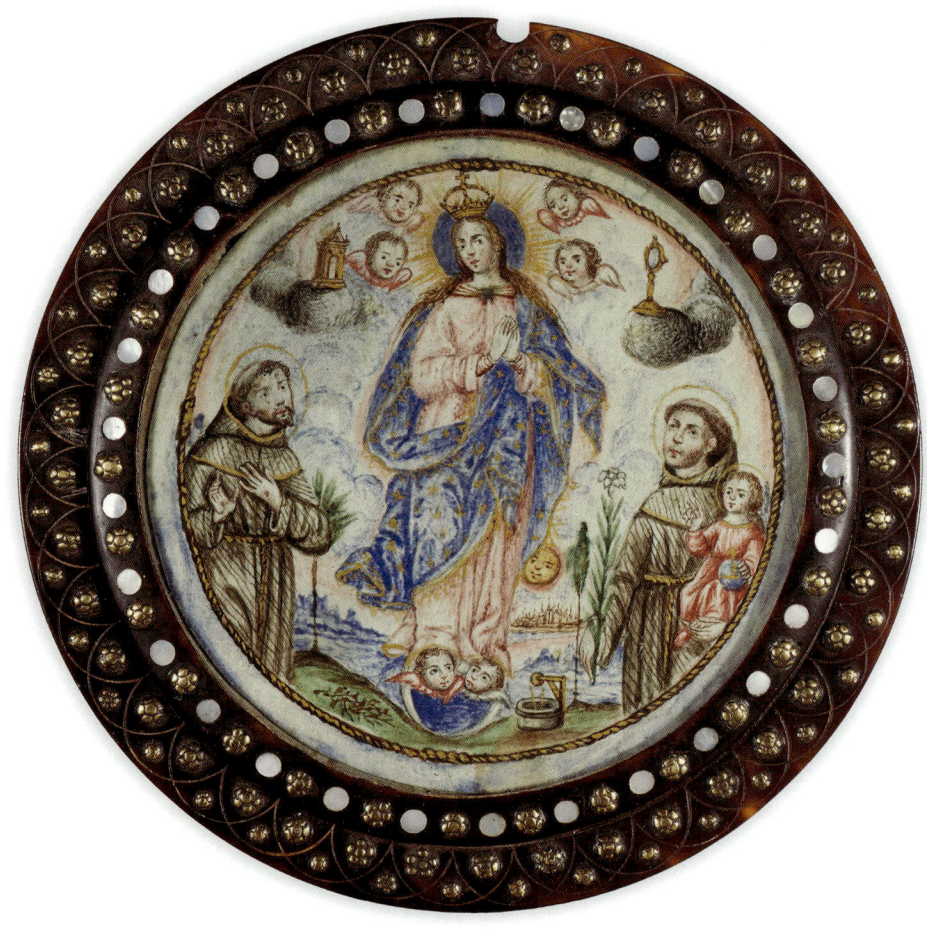

Immaculate Conception with Saints Anthony of Padua and Francis of Assisi

Mexico, 1600s
Colored pencil and gouache on vellum;
tortoiseshell frame (dated 1707) with
mother-of-pearl and brass
4⅔ in. diameter
Gift of the Collection of Frederick
and Jan Mayer; 2013.362

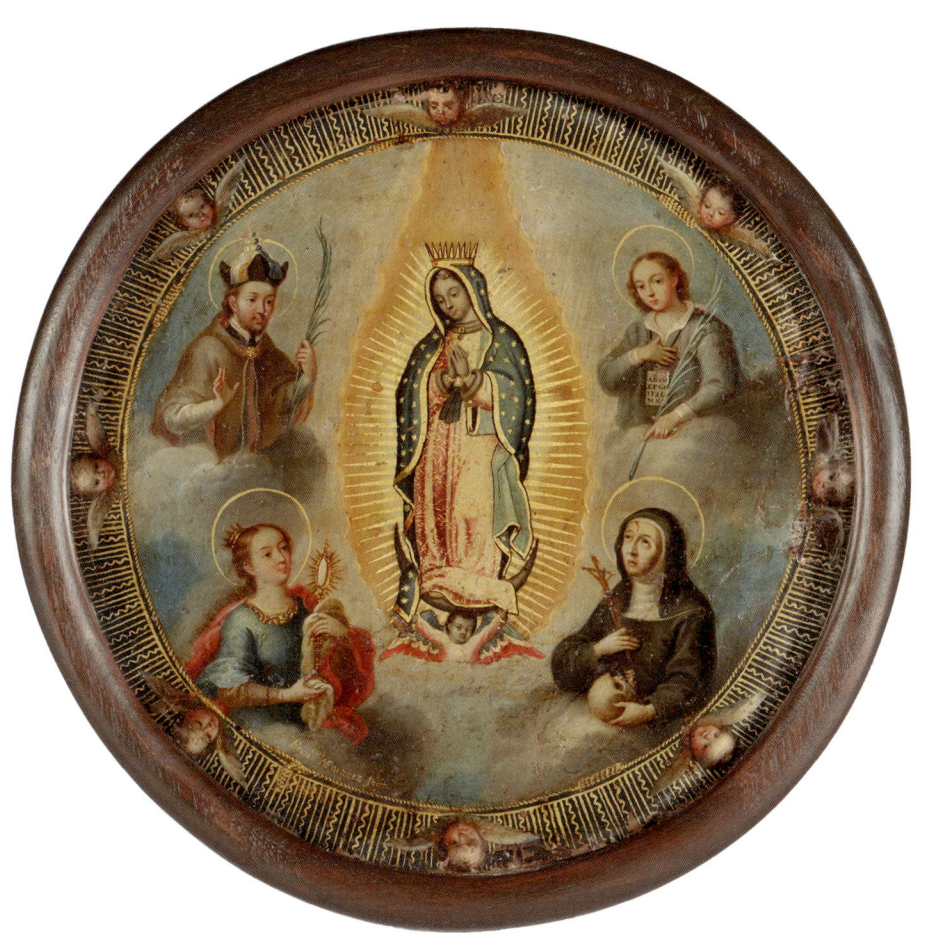

Signed by Francisco Martínez
(active about 1700–1750)

Virgin of Guadalupe
Surrounded by Saints

Mexico, 1700s
Oil and gold leaf on copper;
tortoiseshell frame
8⅜ in. diameter
Gift of the Collection of Frederick
and Jan Mayer; 2013.401

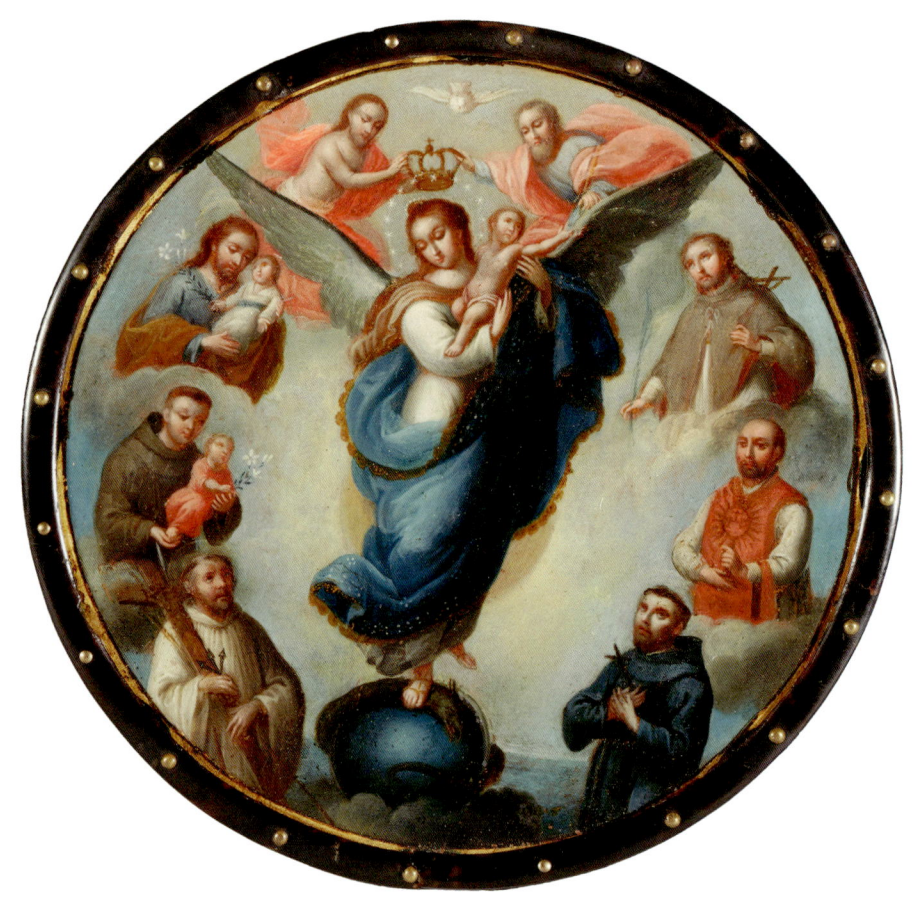

Attributed to
Fray Miguel de Herrera
(about 1725–1780)

*Virgin of the Apocalypse
Surrounded by Saints*

Mexico, 1700s
Oil paint on copper;
tortoiseshell frame
7¼ in. diameter
Funds from Acquisition Challenge
Grant and 1985 Trip Benefit; 1985.361

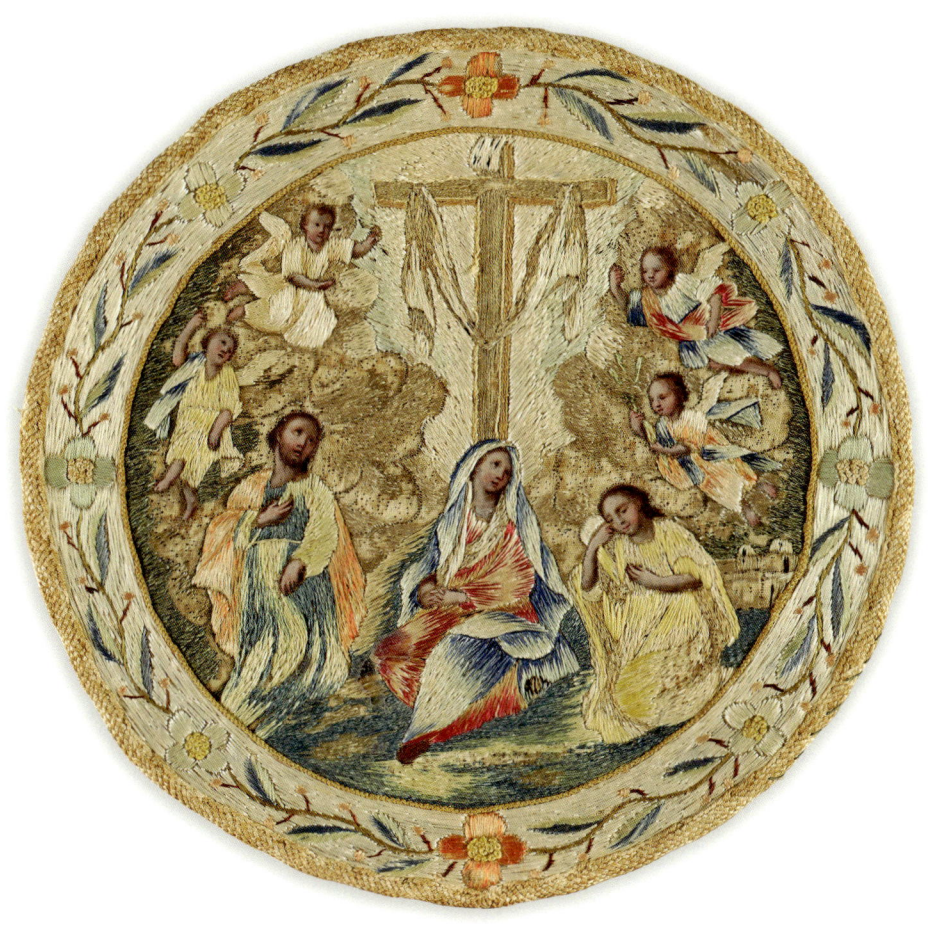

*Virgin of Sorrows with
Saints John the Evangelist
and Mary Magdalene*

Mexico, 1700s
Paint and embroidery on silk
6⅓ in. diameter
Gift of the Collection of Frederick
and Jan Mayer; 2013.360

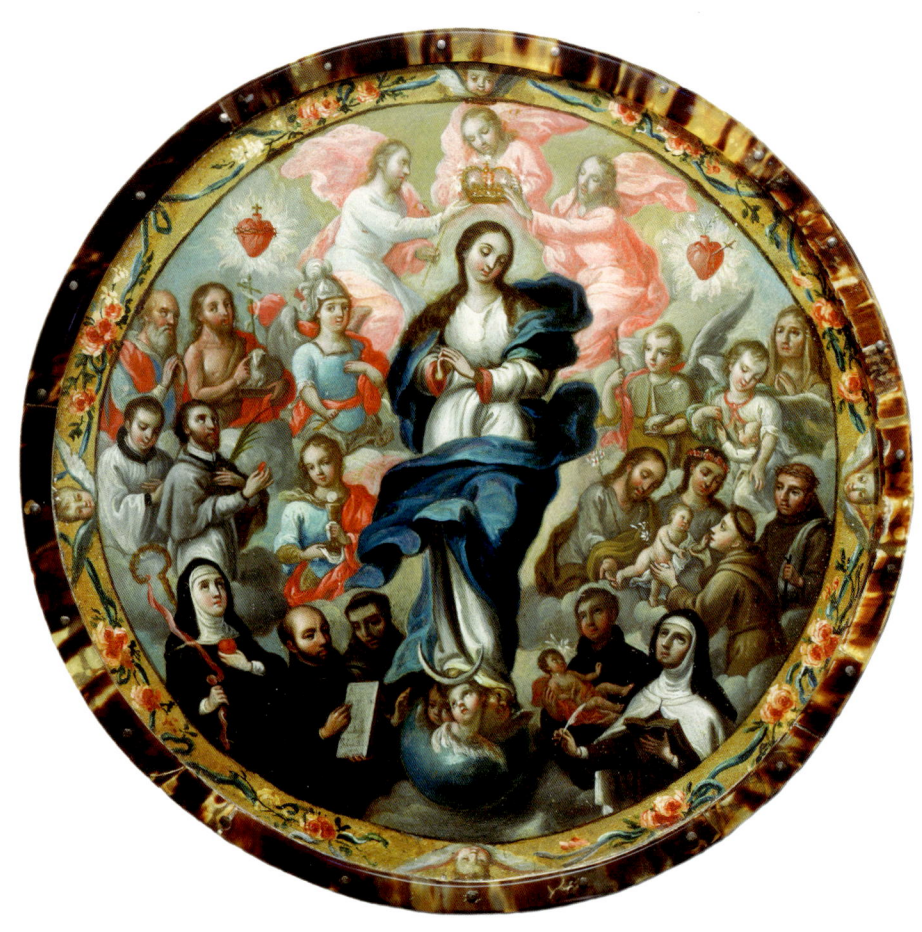

Attributed to
José de Páez
(1720–after 1790)

*Coronation of the Virgin
Surrounded by Saints*

Mexico, 1700s
Oil paint and gold leaf on copper;
tortoiseshell frame
8¼ in. diameter
Collection of Frederick and Jan Mayer;
26.1993

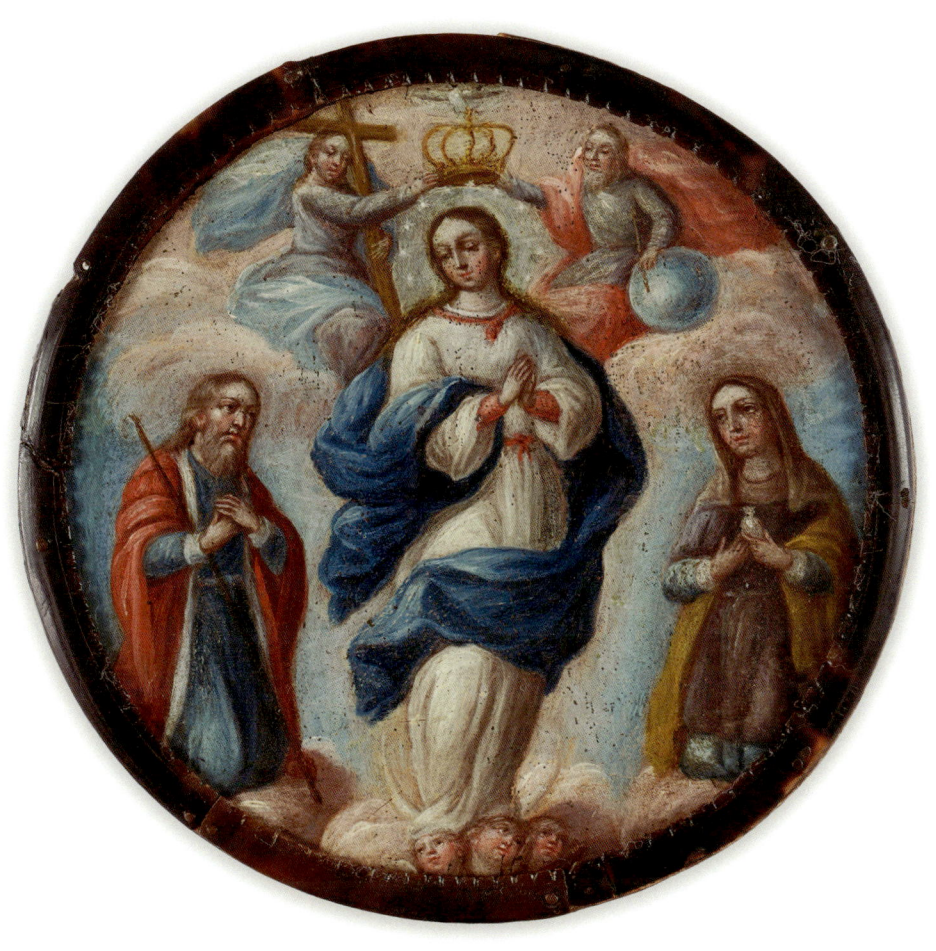

*Coronation of the Virgin with
Saints Anne and Joachim*

Mexico, 1700s
Oil paint on copper;
tortoiseshell frame
4 in. diameter
Gift of the Collection of Frederick
and Jan Mayer; 2013.359

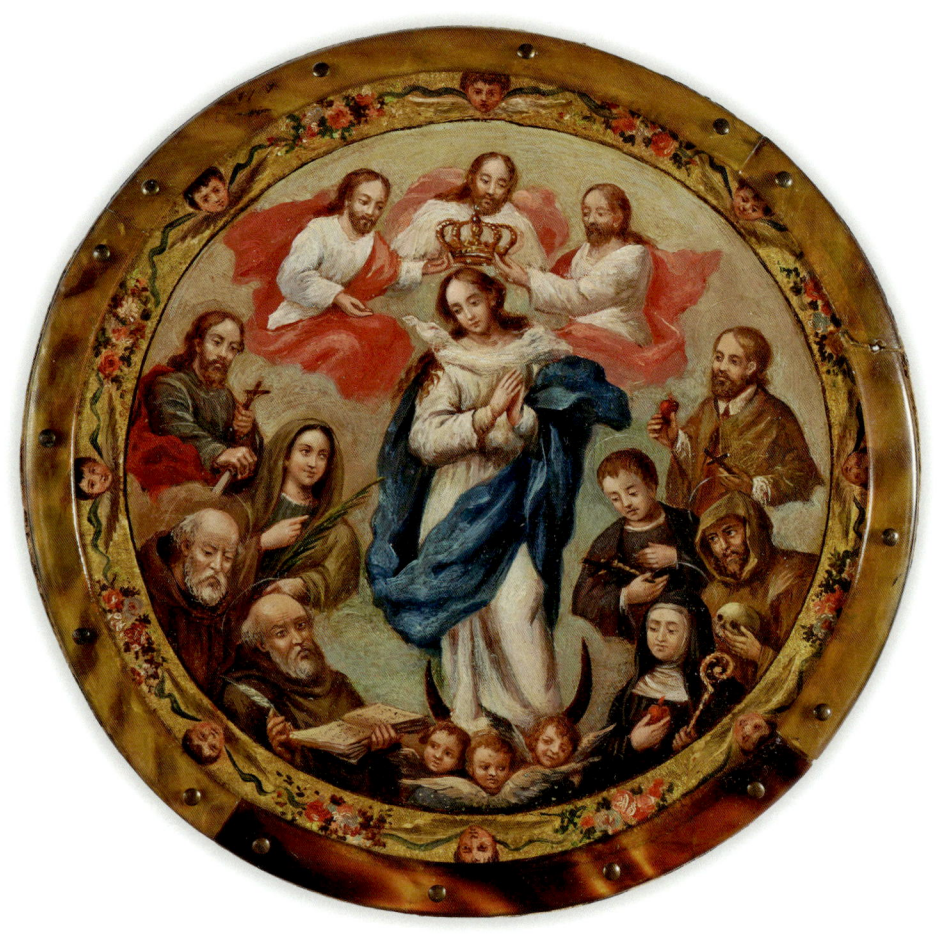

Attributed to Andrés López
(active 1763–1811)

*Coronation of the Virgin
Surrounded by Saints*

Mexico, 1700s
Oil paint and gold leaf on copper;
tortoiseshell frame
7¼ in. diameter
Gift of the Collection of Frederick
and Jan Mayer; 2013.361

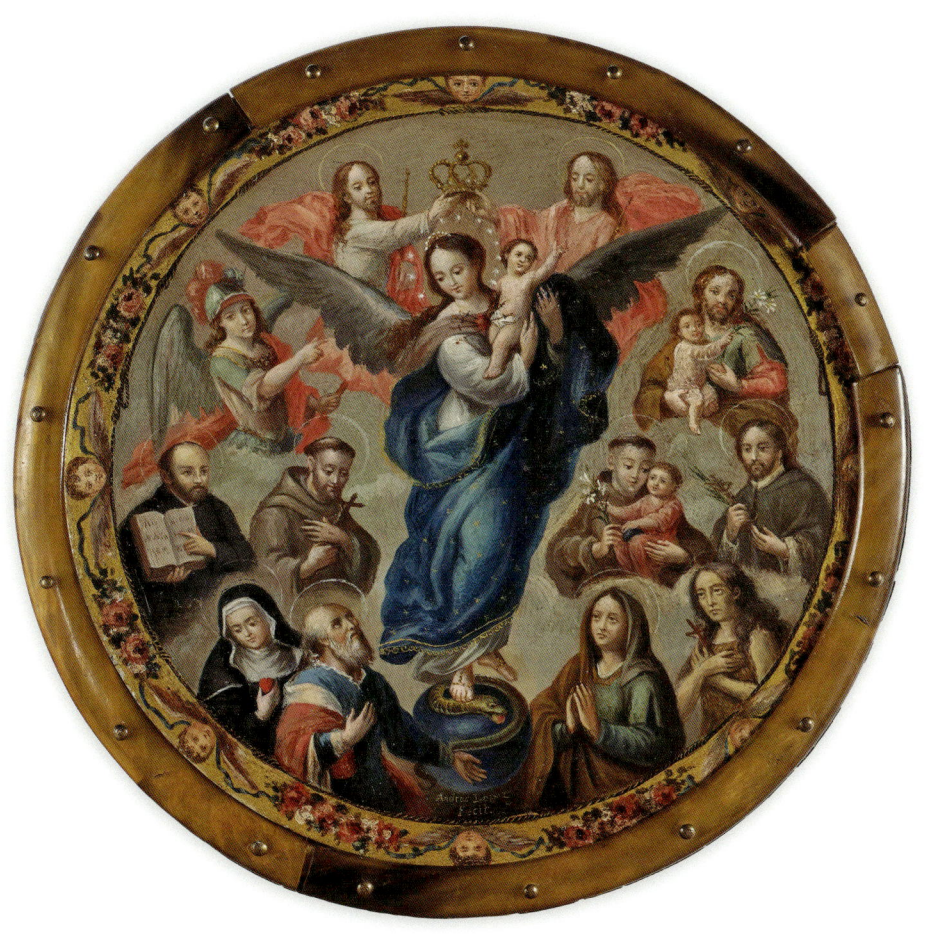

Signed by Andrés López
(active 1763–1811)

*Virgin of the Apocalypse
Surrounded by Saints*

Mexico, 1700s
Oil paint and gold leaf on copper;
tortoiseshell frame
8¼ in. diameter
Gift of the Collection of Frederick
and Jan Mayer; 2013.364

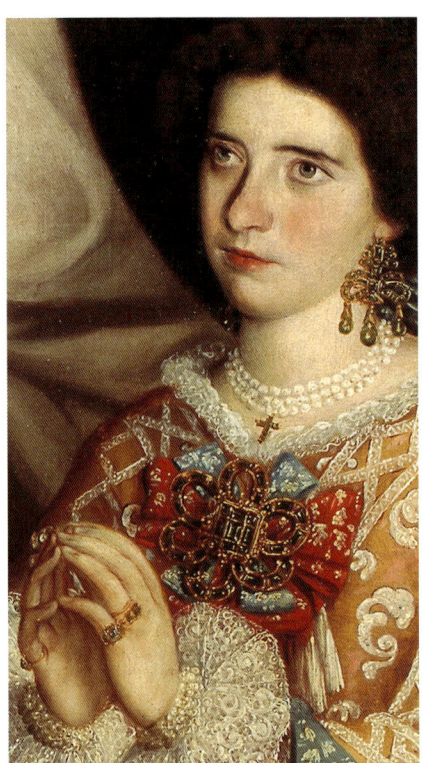

(opposite, and detail left)

Juan Rodríguez Juárez (1675–1728)

St. Rose of Lima with Christ Child and Donor Figure

Mexico, about 1700
Oil paint on canvas
66 x 42 in.
Gift of the Collection of Frederick and Jan Mayer; 2014.216

Paintings often show saints wearing period jewelry. In this rather modest example, Saint Rose of Lima (1586–1617), who was the first saint born in the New World and who lived her entire life in Lima, Peru, wears a subtle band of rose thorns around her forehead in imitation of Christ's crown of thorns. She also wears a rosary of large wooden or jet beads.

In contrast, the donor portrait at lower right depicts a young Mexican woman wearing an opulent dress of metallic-thread brocade over a lace-trimmed chemise. Her elaborate jewelry, typical of the upper classes in Spain and Mexico around 1700, consists of emeralds and pearls set into gold (similar to the cross seen on page 23). She wears multiple rings, a large breast brooch, a multistrand necklace with pendant cross, and extravagant bow-knot earrings, a common motif of Baroque jewelry.

The young woman may have become a nun shortly after this painting was executed. If so, she would have had to relinquish her earthly jewels.

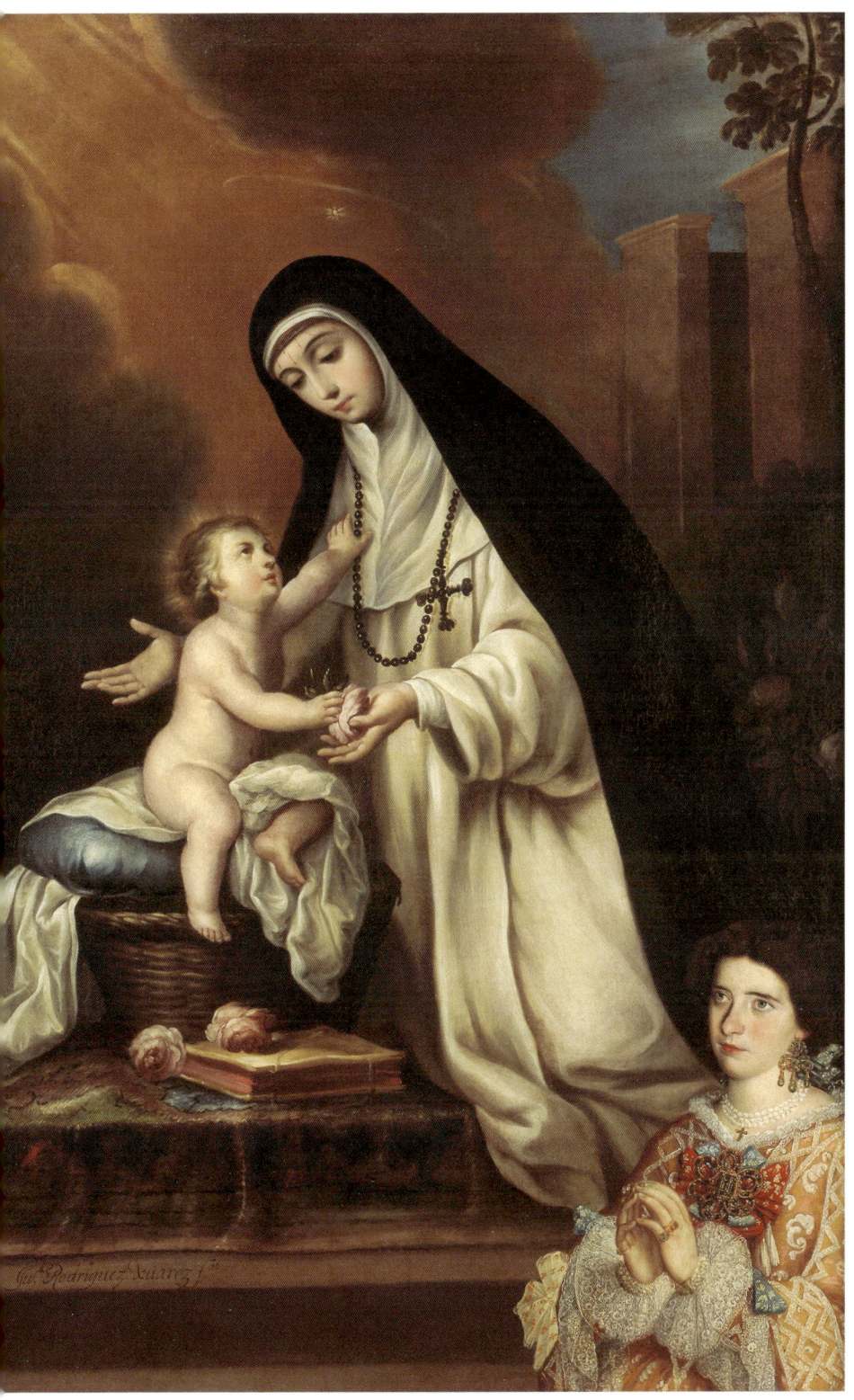

SOURCES CITED

Hernán Cortés: Letters from Mexico, trans. and ed. Anthony R. Padgen, with an introduction by J. H. Elliott (New Haven and London: Yale Univ. Press, 1986), 100–101.

Fanny Calderón de la Barca, *Life in Mexico: Letters of Fanny Calderón de la Barca*, ed. Howard T. and Marion Hall Fisher (1843; reprint, New York: Doubleday, 1966), 138.

Albrecht Dürer, as quoted by Ferdinand Anders, "Las artes menores," *Artes de México* 17, no. 137 (1970), 46. Translation by Donna Pierce.

Thomas Gage, *Thomas Gage's Travels in the New World*, ed. J. Eric S. Thompson (Norman: Univ. of Oklahoma Press, 1985), 71–73.

This publication accompanies the exhibition *Glitterati: Portraits and Jewelry from Colonial Latin America*, on view at the Denver Art Museum December 6, 2014–November 27, 2016.

Published by the Mayer Center for Pre-Columbian and Spanish Colonial Art at the Denver Art Museum © 2015 Denver Art Museum

ISBN 978-0-914738-75-6

Library of Congress Control Number 2015916497

Edited by Laura Caruso
Project management, design, and production by Julie Wilson Frick
Printed by O'Neil Printing, Phoenix, Arizona
Bound by Roswell Bookbinding, Phoenix, Arizona
Distributed to the trade by the University of Oklahoma Press

All photogaphs by Jeff Wells or Christina Jackson, except pages 80–81.

FRONT COVER
Juan Rodríguez Juárez, *St. Rose of Lima with Christ Child and Donor Figure* (detail), see overall page 93

INSIDE FRONT COVER, INSIDE BACK COVER
Portrait of Francisco de Orense y Moctezuma, Count of Villalobos (details), see overall page 33

Dimensions are listed in the following order:
Height x Width x Depth or Diameter.

All works of art pictured within are part of the Denver Art Museum collection, unless otherwise noted.

ISBN: 978-0-914738-75-6